Lectures

in the

Structure of

English

Second Edition

Robert S. Carlisle

California State University, Bakersfield.

Kendall Hunt
publishing company

Cover image © Shutterstock, Inc.

Figures 1--4 courtesy of Ohio State University

Kendall Hunt
publishing company

www.kendallhunt.com
Send all inquiries to:
4050 Westmark Drive
Dubuque, IA 52004-1840

Printed in the United States of America
10 9 8 7 6 5 4 3 2 1

Contents

Lectures in Syntax

Introduction to the Structure of English

Unlearning What You Know

- If your last experience with English grammar was in high school, you will need to unlearn much of what you were taught.
- Definitions in high school textbooks are either incorrect or actually misleading.
- Few teachers, even English teachers, have adequate training in the structure of English.

Unlearning What You Know

- Also, textbooks and teachers concentrate on prescriptive rules of English, which may convince students that they are writing ungrammatical sentences on papers when they are actually making a stylistic choice.
  - For example, ending a sentence in a preposition in English is not ungrammatical in spite of what you have previously learned.

Unlearning What You Know

- Other absurdities include not beginning a sentence with <u>because</u> and not splitting an infinitive.
- Many of these prescriptive rules were misguidedly incorporated into English from Latin in the 18th century.

Unlearning What You Know

- Rules from Latin have no place in English at all because the two languages are entirely different.
- The poor teaching of English grammar and the unwise focus on prescriptivism has given students a poor attitude towards the study of grammar, just as poor as that of a speaker in one of Shakespeare's plays.

Thou hast most traitorously corrupted the youth of the realm in erecting a grammar school....It will be proved to thy face that thou hast men about thee that usually talk of a noun and a verb and such abominable words as no Christian ear can endure to hear.

From   *The Second Part of King Henry the Sixth*

What is a Noun?

- That a noun refers to a person, place, thing, or idea is an antiquated idea.
  - <u>Redness</u> is a natural quality.
  - <u>Depravity</u> is a human quality.
  - <u>Hate</u> is an emotion.
  - <u>Destruction</u> is an action.
  - <u>Earthquake</u> is a natural disaster.
  - <u>Rock concert</u> is a man-made disaster.

_____

What is a Noun?

- A noun is a person, place, thing, idea, natural quality, human quality, emotion, action, natural disaster, or man-made disaster.
- This definition is a notional definition that has no place in linguistics.
- The members of a word class cannot be united under a vague notion of shared meaning.

_____

What is a Noun?

- Words are in the same class if they share morphological and syntactic characteristics.
- What can you do to the following nouns:
  - book   store
  - car   article
  - lawyer   essay
  - brick   stamp

_____

What is a Noun?

- Any word that can be pluralized is a noun, but not all nouns can be pluralized.
- Children understand the concept of plurality.
- Find the nouns:
  - The bellicose cat bit the slothful dog.

What is a Noun?

- Words that can be modified by numerals and/or have a plural form are count nouns.
  - The 'or' is included above because some nouns can be modified by numerals but do not have a plural form: <u>sheep</u>, <u>deer</u>, and <u>moose</u>.
- Count nouns are by far the most frequent type of noun in English, comprising at least 85% of all nouns.

What is a Noun?

- A much smaller category of noun is the proper noun. Such nouns refer to unique entities and are capitalized in English.
- What can you do to these proper nouns?
  - Tom
  - Nancy
  - Napoleon
  - Caesar

What is a Noun?

- Almost all proper nouns can have a possessive form.
  - Tom's first class
  - Nancy's friends
  - Napoleon's last battle
  - Caesar's final days

_____

_____

_____

_____

_____

What is a Noun?

- Any word that can be made plural or possessive is a noun, but not all nouns can be made plural or possessive, such as the following.
  - happiness
  - tennis
  - linguistics
  - haste

_____

_____

_____

_____

_____

What is a Noun?

- Words such as happiness, tennis, linguistics, and haste are called mass or non-count nouns.
- They are a very small class of nouns, and a later lecture will provide more information about how to recognize them.

_____

_____

_____

_____

_____

What is a Verb?

- Traditionally, a verb has been called an action word. What are the actions below?
  - Tom <u>appears</u> tired.
  - Jess <u>owns</u> a jeep.
  - Mario <u>has</u> a cold.
  - The class <u>seems</u> indifferent.
  - The children <u>sleep</u> for about eight hours.
  - Dan Quayle <u>is</u> a great speller.

_____

_____

_____

_____

_____

_____

What is a Verb?

- What can you do to these verbs?
  - talk
  - jump
  - irrigate
  - mix
  - fulfill

_____

_____

_____

_____

_____

_____

What is a Verb?

- The verbs on the previous slide all have past tense forms:

talk	talked
jump	jumped
irrigate	irrigated
mix	mixed
fulfill	fulfilled

_____

_____

_____

_____

_____

_____

_____

What is a Verb?

- A verb is a word that changes form for changes in tense.
- Find the verb in these sentences.
  - The dogs eat canned food.
  - The post office closes at noon.
  - The Smiths jog in the park.
  - The instructor assigns a term paper.

What is a Verb?

- Now read the same sentences after putting the word <u>yesterday</u> in front of each.
  - The dogs eat canned food.
  - The post office closes at noon.
  - The Smiths jog in the park.
  - The instructor assigns a term paper.

What is a Pronoun?

- Old definitions state that a pronoun takes the place of a noun.
- Look at the noun in the following sentence.
  - The corpulent <u>elephant</u> died.
  - The corpulent <u>it</u> died.
  - <u>It</u> died.

What is a Pronoun?

- Pronouns substitute for noun phrases.
  - <u>The man in the striped shirt who tried to eat a pound of squid with chopsticks</u> turned as blue as ink.
  - <u>He</u> turned as blue as ink.

What is a Conjunction?

- A conjunction links words or phrases.
  - <u>Bush</u> and <u>Quayle</u> are ideological clones.
  - We exercise <u>at the gym</u> or <u>in the park</u>.
  - The students are <u>happy</u> and <u>content</u>.
  - *George is <u>a student</u> and <u>in the library</u>.

What is a Conjunction?

- A conjunction links phrases of equal grammatical structure.
  - Nancy read a book <u>on the Roman empire</u>.
  - Nancy read a book <u>on the couch</u>.
  - *Nancy read a book <u>on the Roman empire</u> and <u>on the couch</u>.

What is a Conjunction?

- A conjunction links phrases of equal grammatical structure and equal grammatical function.
  - Nancy reads books on the Roman empire and on theoretical linguistics.
  - Nancy reads in her room and at the library.

_____

_____

_____

_____

_____

_____

The Components of Language

Language

Phonology   Morphology   Syntax

_____

_____

_____

_____

_____

_____

Lectures
in
Phonetics
and
Phonology

Introduction to Phonology

Articulatory Phonetics

Handwritten notes:
Articulatory language –
Human speech sounds are produced

What is Phonology?

- Phonology is the sound system of a language.
  - An inventory of sounds.
    - Language specific inventory
  - Conditions for combining sounds
    - Phonotactics
  - Rules for pronouncing sounds in particular phonological environments.
    - Phonological rules

Handwritten notes:
pronunciation
- 120 sounds in universal language

A Few Basics

- Human speech sounds are produced through the movement of the air stream through the vocal tract.
  - The vocal tract consists of the glottis, the pharynx, the oral cavity, and the nasal cavity.
- The airstream is modified at different locations in the vocal tract.
- Different sounds result when a change along any of three parameters occurs.

Handwritten notes:
egressive sounds – most sounds
- different sounds result where the airstream is modified in different locations in the vocal tract

The First Parameter

- The first parameter for describing the production of sounds is the state of the glottis.
  - The glottis is the area between the vocal folds in the larynx.
  - The glottis has a number of different states that produce different sounds.
  - Three states are important for the production of English sounds.

voiceless

voiced

whisper

States of the Glottis: Voiceless

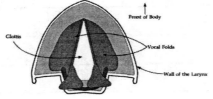

Figure 1. Open Vocal Folds

— produced when
  vocal chords
  don't vibrate
—S voiceless
  no vibration in
  throat

States of the Glottis: Voiced

Figure 2. Appproximated Vocal folds

— vibration
— sounds produced w/
  vibration
—z vibration

closed
— Pressure builds
  up underneath them

States of the Glottis: Whisper

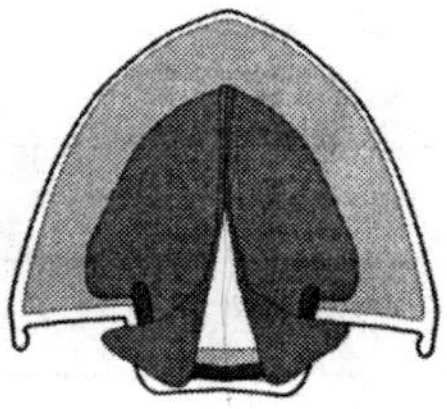

Figure 3. Partially Closed Vocal Folds

- allows air to espace prvenk vocal vibrating

- nothing more than controlling your vocal chords they don't vibrate

Practice

- Identify the state of the glottis for the following sounds.
  - /b/ voiced ✓
  - /m/ voiced ✓
  - /f/ voiceless ✓
  - /l/ voiced ✓
  - /t/ voiceless ✓
  - /r/ voiced ✓

- put hand to throat

The First Parameter

- Some consonants differ from each other only in voicing.
- Another way of saying this is that some consonants are in voiced and voiceless pairs.
- All vowels are voiced.

Practice

- Below is a list of voiced sounds; discover the voiceless counterpart.
  - /b/ p
  - /d/ t
  - /g/ k
  - /v/ f
  - /z/ s

The Second Parameter

- The second parameter for the production of speech sounds is place of articulation.
  - The place of articulation is that point in the oral cavity where maximal constriction occurs.
  - The airstream is modified at the site of maximal constriction.
  - Constriction takes place because two articulators either touch--forming occlusion--or approximate *very close to each other* each other. Boy   s

B - the lips touch
S - the tongue comes very
close to the alveolar ridge
doesn't touch

The Second Parameter

- The following slide contains a sagittal section of the vocal tract.
- Use this slide to follow the lecture on the places of articulation.

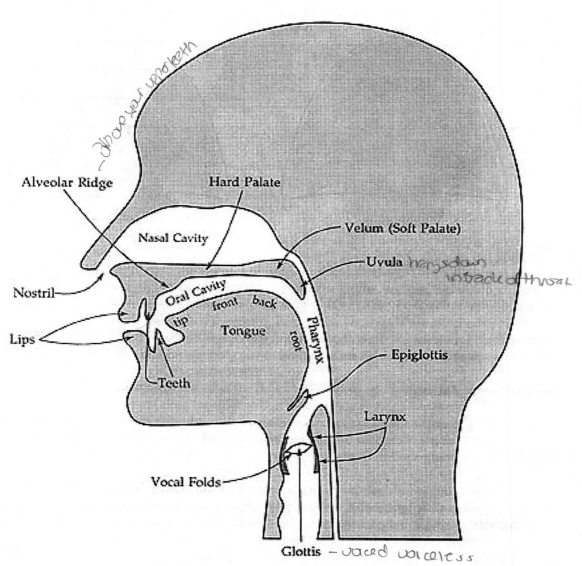

Figure 4.   Sagittal section of the vocal tract.

The Second Parameter

- There are two sets of articulators: the lower articulators and the upper articulators.
- The lower articulators are also called the mobile articulators because they move towards the upper articulators
  - lower lip
  - lower teeth
  - tongue

The Second Parameter

- The upper articulators are also called the stationary articulators because they do not move.
  - glottis   pharyngeal wall
  - uvula   palate
  - alveolar ridge   alveo-palatal region
  - upper teeth   upper lip

The Second Parameter

- Places of articulation in English.
  - Glottal sounds are produced at the glottis. The airstream is modified at the vocal folds.
    - /h/ as in hurt is a glottal sound.
  - Velar sounds are made at the velum with the back of the tongue.
    - English has three velar sounds: /k/ as in core, /g/ as in go, and /ŋ/ as in sting.

18

The Second Parameter

– Palatal sounds are made at the palate with the center of the tongue.
  • The only palatal sound is English is /j/ as in yes.
– Alveopalatal sounds are produced in the area immediately behind the alveolar ridge with the front of the tongue.
  • English has four alveopalatal sounds: /š/ or /ʃ/ as in shore, /ž/ or /ʒ/ as in azure, /č/ or /tʃ/ as in chat, and /ǰ/ or /dʒ/ as in juice.

any time you see 2 *tongue* over the sound you no they are Alveopal atal

The Second Parameter

– Alveolar sounds are produced at the alveolar ridge with the tip or the blade of the tongue.
  • English has a large number of alveolar sounds. Below are examples of some of them:
    – /t/ as in time
    – /s/ as in sun
    – /n/ as in no and know
    – /l/ as in lost
    – /d/ as in doughnut

The Second Parameter

– Labiodental sounds are produced at the upper front teeth with the lower lip.
  • English as two labiodental sounds: /f/ as in fat and /v/ as in vat.
– Interdental sounds are produced between the front teeth with the tip or blade of the tongue.
  • English has two interdental sounds: /θ/ as in thin and /ð/ as in then.

The Second Parameter

- Bilabial sounds are produced at the upper lip with the lower lip.
  - English had three bilabial sounds:
    - /b/ as in <u>base</u>
    - /p/ as in <u>pace</u>
    - /m/ as in <u>mace</u>

The Second Parameter

- Vowels and place of articulation.
  - In the production of vowels, none of the articulators approximate one another very closely.
  - The oral cavity is relatively unobstructed.
  - Vowel sounds will be described according to the relative position of tongue in the oral cavity.

- production of constants
not really vowels

Practice

- Produce the following sounds and determine their place of articulation.
  - /s/ *alvelar*
  - /f/ *libiodental*
  - /b/ *bilabial*
  - /k/ *vela*
  - /t/ *avelar*
  - /h/ *Glottal*

The Third Parameter

- The third parameter for the production of speech sounds is manner of articulation.
  - Manner of articulation is how the airstream is modified as it moves through the vocal tract.
  - Two sounds can be identical in voicing and place of articulation, but still have different qualities because they differ in manner of articulation.

s and t = voiceles
alveolar
diff sounds thagh so we
need articulate them manner
of articulation, how the air is
released

The Third Parameter

- For example, /t/ is voiceless and alveolar; /s/ is also voiceless and alveolar, but they are distinct sounds.
- Obviously, at least one more parameter is necessary if we are to distinguish /t/ from /s/.
- This parameter is manner of articulation.

The Third Parameter

- Manners of articulation in English.
- The first three groups of consonants are all known as obstruents because they are made with a great deal of obstruction.
  - Stops
    - Two articulators form occlusion at some point in the oral cavity.
    - Air pressure builds up behind the occlusion.
    - The articulators are released suddenly.

groups of conants
touch or very close together
p t k - voiceles
b d g - voiced   } stops

The Third Parameter

- English has six stops:
  - /p/ as in post
  - /t/ as in tan
  - /k/ as in cool
  - /b/ as in bother
  - /d/ as in dust
  - /g/ as in ghoul (don't be fooled by spelling)

The Third Parameter

- Fricatives
  - Two articulators closely approximate each other forming a narrow passage.
  - The airstream is forced through the passage producing a turbulent airflow.
  - English has nine fricatives:

/s/ is example
can make africative long as long
as you have air in your lungs
narrow passage

The Third Parameter

- /θ/ as in fourth
- /ð/ as in this
- /f/ as in staff
- /v/ as in visor
- /s/ as in horse
- /z/ as in zoo
- /ʃ/ as in hash
- /ʒ/ as in measure
- /h/ as in hurt

The Third Parameter

– Affricates
- Two articulators form complete occlusion at some point in the oral cavity.
- The articulators are released more gradually than they are for stops, resulting in a turbulent airflow.
- Affricates begin like stops and end like fricatives.

The Third Parameter

- Afficates
  – English has two affricates;
    - /tʃ/ as in chip and match
    - /dʒ/ as in joy and fudge

The Third Parameter

- The next four categories of sounds are made with little turbulence in the airflow and are known as sonorants. not produced by any friction
  – Nasals
    - Like stops, nasals are made with occlusion in the oral cavity. complete blockage
  - Velic closure is released.
  - The airflow escapes through the nasal cavity.

velic closure – airean escape through nasal

The Third Parameter

- English has thee nasals:
  - /m/ as in <u>more</u> and <u>some</u>
  - /n/ as in <u>note</u> and <u>stone</u>
  - /ŋ/ as in <u>song</u>
    - Note that /ŋ/ appears only after vowels in English, never before.

The Third Parameter

- Liquids
  - Two articulators approach each other, but not enough to produce a turbulent airflow.
  - A retroflex is produced with the back of the tongue slightly arched towards the alveolar ridge. The airflow escapes around both sides of the tongue.
  - A lateral is made with occlusion at the alveolar ridge. One side of the tongue is lowered, allowing the airflow to escape.

The Third Parameter

- English has two liquids:
  - /r/ as in <u>rip</u> and <u>star</u>
  - /l/ as in <u>lip</u> and <u>stall</u>
    - Note that even though <u>stall</u> is written with two <u>l</u> characters, it is pronounced with a single /l/ sound.

The Third Parameter

– Glides
- Two articulators are quite distant form each other.
- The distance is similar to that for the production of vowels.
- Sometimes glides are called semi-vowels or semi-consonants.
- Glides are always associated with a vowel; they either "glide on" to the vowel or "glide off."

by vowel   after vowel

immediately b4 a vowel
or after a vowel

The Third Parameter

- English has two glides /w/ and /j/.
  – /w/ is a labial velar glide and appears in words such as we, west and bough.
  – /j/ is a palatal glide and appears in words such as yes, yam and toy.

Practice

- Produce the following sounds and determine their manner of articulation.
  – /s/ alveolar, fricative
  – /t/ stop, alveolar
  – /v/ fricative, labiodental
  – /m/ bilabial, nasal
  – /l/ lateral liquid, alveolar
  – /d/ stop, alveolar

The Third Parameter

– Vowels   *son orants*
  - Vowels are produced with less obstruction than are any other sounds in a language.
  - The airflow is not turbulent. *more room for air to escape*
  - Vowels will be described according to the height of the tongue. *rises & lowers*
  - Vowels will be described according to the advancement of the tongue.
    forward & Backward

_____

_____

_____

_____

_____

_____

_____

speech video

- the machine allows us to see a side view of the mouth
- the seperation of the oral & nasal cavities

The Sounds of English

*All sounds of english,
every single sound has a
unique description*

The Sounds of English

- The phonology of a language must have an inventory of sounds.
- The two basic groups of sounds are consonants and vowels.
- Each of these groups is described along certain parameters.
- The parameters for describing the two sets of sounds differ from each other.

height

The Parameters for Describing Consonants

- The state of the glottis.
  - Voiced *vocal vibration*
  - Voiceless *no vocal vibration*
- Place of articulation.
  - Which articulators are involved in the production of the consonants. *where is the sound produced in mouth*
- Manner of articulation.
  - How the air is released.

The Consonants of English

- The Stops of English
  - /p/   VL   bilabial   stop
  - /t/   VL   alveolar   stop
  - /k/   VL   velar   stop
  - /b/   VD   bilabial   stop
  - /d/   VD   alveolar   stop
  - /g/   VD   velar   stop

The Consonants of English

- The affricates of English
  - /tʃ/   VL   alveopalatal   affricate   *chat*
  - /dʒ/   VD   alveopalatal   affricate   *judge*

only alveopalatal have ✓ over the letters

The Consonants of English

- The voiceless fricatives of English
  - /θ/   VL   interdental   fricative   *thin*   (theta)
  - /f/   VL   labiodental   fricative   *Frank*
  - /s/   VL   alveolar   fricative   *Sam*
  - /ʃ/   VL   alveopalatal   fricative   *short marsh*
  - /h/   VL   glottal   fricative

there's no voiced counterpart in /h/

The Consonants of English

- **The voiced fricatives of English**

eta	– /ð/	VD	interdental	fricative
	– /v/	VD	labiodental	fricative
	– /z/	VD	alveolar	fricative
ǯ	– /ʒ/	VD	alveopalatal	fricative

(handwritten) this that them there the
(handwritten) vote
(handwritten) zoo
(handwritten) mea**sure**

The Consonants of English

- **The nasals of English**

	– /m/	VD	bilabial	nasal
	– /n/	VD	alveolar	nasal
eng	– /ŋ/	VD	velar	nasal

(handwritten) no
(handwritten) sti**ng**
(handwritten) occurs only after vowels

The Consonants of English

- **The liquids of English**

	– /l/	VD	alveolar	lateral liquid
	– /r/	VD	alveolar	retroflex liquid

(handwritten) lost
(handwritten) rust

- **The glides of English**

	– /w/	VD	labial velar	glide
y	– /j/	VD	palatal	glide

(handwritten) 2 places of articulation west
(handwritten) yes
(handwritten) tongue rises toward palat

The Vowels of English

- Unlike consonants, vowels are produced with a minimal amount of constriction.
  - The vocal tract is relatively open. *minimal amount of constriction*
- All vowels in English are voiced.
- Different vowel qualities are produced by changes in the configuration of the vocal tract.

1st The Parameters for Describing Vowels

- Height of Tongue
  - The tongue is raised to different levels to produce vowels.
  - There are three traditionally recognized levels of vowel height: high, mid, and low.
    - /i/ high   *e sound beat*
    - /e/ mid   *a sound bait*
    - /æ/ low   *a sound hat*
         short a

raise drops changing between each vowel

2nd The Parameters for Describing Vowels

- Tongue Advancement
  - The normal resting position of the tongue is in the mid central part of the mouth.
  - Vowels at the front or back of the mouth are made by fronting or retracting the tongue.
  - There are three traditionally recognized degrees of tongue advancement: front, central and back.
    - /i/ front   /ʌ/ central   /u/ back   *all high position*
       e beat   shrt u   · boot
              cut

resting
move forward or
move backward

3rd The Parameters for Describing Vowels

- **Tenseness**
  - Some vowels are made by fronting or retracting the tongue.
  - Some of these vowels are more peripheral than others meaning that the tongue is extended even further. To reach these peripheral positions the tongue must become tense.
  - English has four tense vowels: /i/, /e/, /u/ and /o/.

beat bait boot boat

tongue must become tense

4th The Parameters for Describing Vowels

- **Rounding**
  - Some vowels in English are produced with rounding of the lips.
  - These rounded vowels in English are the non-low back vowels.
    - /u/ boot
    - /ʊ/ could
    - /o/ boat
    - /ɔ/ caught found in west coast w/ accent

cannot round w?

mid or high back vowels

The Simple Vowels of English

- The simple vowels are formed by the tongue going to a particular position and remaining there fleetingly during the production of the vowel.
- Simple vowels are formed differently than are the diphthongs, which will be described shortly.
- The following slides displays the relative positions of the simple vowels of English.
- Following slides will contain descriptions of all the vowels and provide examples words containing them.

Simple Vowels

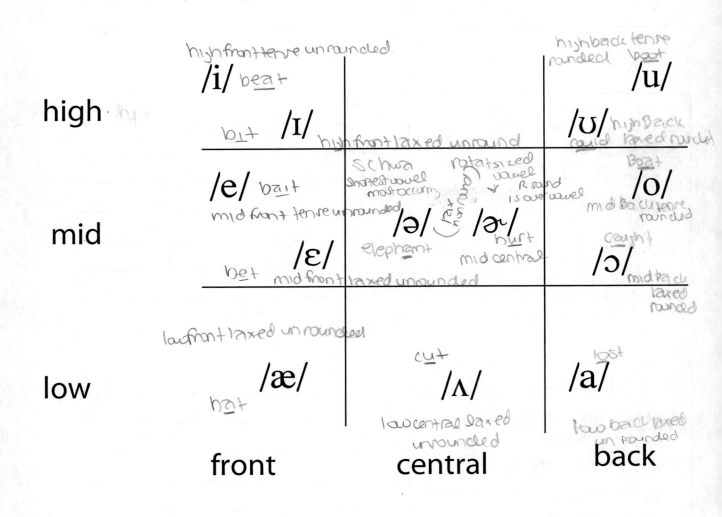

high front tense unrounded

/i/ b<u>ea</u>t

high

b<u>i</u>t /ɪ/ **high front laxed unround**

/e/ b<u>ai</u>t

mid front tense unrounded

mid

/ɛ/

b<u>e</u>t **mid front laxed unrounded**

Schwa
shortest vowel
most occurs

rotatorized vowel
↓
R sound is over vowel

/ə/ **(rat hers)** /ɚ/
el<u>e</u>phant h<u>u</u>rt
mid central

high back tense rounded b<u>oo</u>t

/u/

/ʊ/ **high back could laxed rounded**

B<u>oa</u>t
/o/
mid back tense rounded

c<u>augh</u>t
/ɔ/
mid back laxed rounded

low front laxed unrounded

c<u>u</u>t

low

/æ/

h<u>a</u>t

/ʌ/

low central laxed unrounded

front

central

l<u>o</u>st

/a/

low back laxed unrounded

back

High Front Vowels

- English has two high front vowels: /i/ and /ɪ/.
  – /i/ is known as long e as in beat and east.
  – /ɪ/ is known as short i as in bit.
- Note that even though both vowels occupy the same quadrant on the vowel chart /i/ is more peripheral, meaning that it is the tense vowel of the pair. Among paired simple vowels, the tense vowels are always the more peripheral.
- /i/ is a high front tense unrounded vowel.
- /ɪ/ is a high front lax unrounded vowel.

_____

_____

_____

_____

_____

_____

Mid Front Vowels

- English has two mid front vowels: /e/ and /ɛ/.
  – /e/ is known as long a as in bait and ace.
  – /ɛ/ is known as short e as in bet.
- Again, /e/ is more peripheral member of the pair, meaning that it is the tense vowel.
- /e/ is a mid front tense unrounded vowel.
- /ɛ/ is a mid front lax unrounded vowel.

_____

_____

_____

_____

_____

_____

Low Front Vowel

- English has only one low front vowel, /æ/, which is called short a.
- Short a appears is words such as bat, after, and Al.
- /æ/ is a low front lax unrounded vowel.
- Short a is not tense because it is the only vowel in the low front quadrant of the vowel chart.
- Also, none of the front or the central vowels (to be discussed next) are round because only non-low back vowels are round in English.

_____

_____

_____

_____

_____

_____

Mid Central Vowels

- As indicated on your vowel chart, English has two mid central vowels. The one further front in the mouth is called schwa and is symbolized as /ə/.
- Schwa is physically the shortest vowel in English and is consequently referred to as a reduced vowel.
- Schwa normally appears in unstressed syllables as in the second syllable in parrot and edible.
- Schwa is a mid central lax reduced unrounded vowel.

Mid Central Vowels

- The second mid central vowel is /ɚ/, which is the rhotacized vowel. Rhotacized means r-colored. That is, an r-like quality is superimposed on the vowel itself.
- For example, /ɚ/ appears in words such as bird, hurt, shirt. When you say these words, you cannot hear a distinction between the vowel and the r-quality.
- In contrast, if you say door slowly, you will clearly hear /o/ before the /r/.
- /ɚ/ is a mid central lax rhotacized unrounded vowel.

r sound covers the vowel sound contactually hear it

Low Central Vowel

- English has only one low central vowel: /ʌ/.
- This vowel is known as short u.
- Short u is a lax unrounded vowel.
- It is found is such words as duck, butter , and under.

High Back Vowels

* English has two high back vowels: /u/ and /ʊ/.
  * /u/ is called long u and appears in words such as youth, shoe and udo.
* /ʊ/ is called horseshoe u and appears in rather few words, but some of those appear with high frequency such as would, should, could and good.
* /u/ is the more peripheral of the two vowels and is tense/
* /u/ is a high back tense rounded vowel.
* /ʊ/ is a high back lax rounded vowel.

Mid Back Vowels

* English has two mid back vowels: /o/ and /ɔ/.
  * /o/ is called long o and appears in words such as oats, ghost and go.
  * /ɔ/ is called open o and may not appear in your dialect. If you say caught and cot as homophones, you do not produce open o; instead you say both words with short o, which appears on the next slide.
* /o/ is more peripheral and consequently is tense.
* /o/ is a mid back tense rounded vowel.
* /ɔ/ is a mid back lax rounded vowel.

ɔ is mainly used in the east coast w/ an accent

Low Back Vowel

* English has one low back vowel: /a/.
  – /a/ is called short o and appears in words such as hop, ought, and saw.
* As mentioned previously, speakers who pronounce pairs such as caught and cot homophonously, have short o, but not open o, in their inventory of vowels.
* Short o is the only back vowel that is not round, and because it is alone is its quadrant , is it also not tense.
* /a/ is a low back lax unrounded vowel.

Complicated vowel sounds

Diphthongs

- A diphthong is a vowel which has a change of vowel quality in the same syllable.
- The change in vowel quality is due to tongue movement from one position to another.
- Where the diphthong begins and ends may not exactly correspond to any simple vowel or to the two glides.

Diphthongs

- The first part of the diphthong is more prominent than the second; it is usually symbolized with the sign of the vowel closest to where it begins.
- The second quality is usually symbolized with the sign of the vowel closest to where it ends or as a glide--/w/ or /j/.
- English has three diphthongs.

The Diphthong /aj/

- The diphthong /aj/ starts in a low back position and ends in a high front position.
- The diphthong may also be symbolized as /ai/.
- Words with /aj/.   long i
  - hide
  - I
  - slight

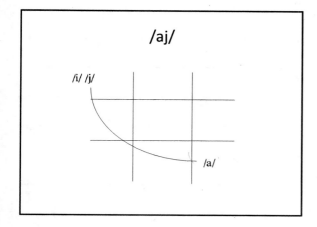

The Diphthong /oj/

- The diphthong /oj/ starts in a mid back position and ends in a high front position.
- The diphthong may also be symbolized as /oi/.
- Words with /oj/.
  - boy
  - voyager
  - hoist

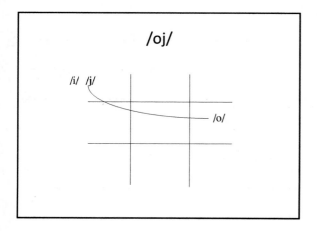

lips are round at beginning
But not at the end

The Diphthong /aw/

- The diphthong /aw/ starts in a low back position and ends in a high back position.
- The diphthong may also be symbolized as /au/.
- Words with /au/.
  - cow
  - about
  - sprout

/aw/

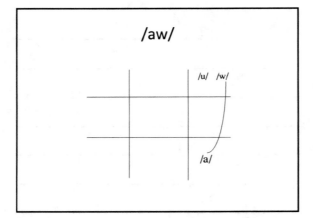

Transcriptions

- Now that you know the symbols for the sounds of English, you can now read passages written with them.
- Open Exercises in the Structure of English, and do the following exercises in class together.
  - Exercise 10
  - Exercise 11
  - Exercise 12

The Phonology of English

The sound system of the language

how the language is pronounced

Phonemes

- Phonemes are the distinctive sounds of a language.
- Sounds are distinctive if a change in sound produces a change in meaning.
  - /bit/ /mit/ /sit/ /nit/ /pit/ /fit/ /tʃit/ /ʃit/
- Each initial sound above is distinctive as it produces a new meaning.
- The rest of the word is identical in each case-- /it/.

Phonemes

- In other words, the initial sounds are in the same environment.
- Phonemes "contrast" in the same environment.
- No two languages have the same inventory of phonemes.
- Phonemes are denoted by placing them in virgules--//.

- *If you change the phonemes change the meaning*
- *everytime you see a virgule you know it is a phoneme*

Minimal Pairs

- The best way to discover the phonemes of a language is to examine them in the context of minimal pairs.
- A minimal pair consists of two words that differ by only one sound which is found in the same location in both words.
  - /bot/ /mot/
  - /nad/ /kad/

Practice

- Which sets of words below are minimal pairs?
  - set   sat *
  - slim   dim   can't compare 4 sounds to 3 sounds
  - tip   pit
  - must   dust *
  - past   best
  - run   fun *

Describing Phonemes

- Each phoneme must be uniquely identified.
- Only those features are used that unambiguously distinguish one phoneme from another.
- Phonemes are therefore described with a minimal amount of detail.

Describing Phonemes

- Consonants essentially need only three features:
  - Voicing
  - Place of articulation
  - Manner of articulation

Practice

- Which sequences of descriptive features below uniquely identify a phoneme.
  - VL stop   3   P T K
  - VD alveolar fricative   Z
  - alveolar fricative   2 doesn't.
  - nasal   3 nasaL in Eng.
  - VL fricative   5 voiceless in Eng

Describing Phonemes

- In general, no two features uniquely identify the consonants of English.
- The articulatory features that distinguish one phoneme from another are called distinctive features.
- A universal inventory of articulatory features exists from which each language selects a subset as its distinctive features.

arthictory feature

1) voicing 2) Place of articulation, 3) manner of articulation

Distinctive Features

- Articulatory features that are distinctive in one language may not be distinctive in another.
- Aspiration is distinctive in Thai.
  - [pʰaa] = to split *aspiration difference*
  - [paa] = forest *voicing*
  - [baa] = shoulder

Distinctive Features

- Aspiration is an articulatory feature of English, but it is not distinctive. *doesn't change meaning*
  - [pʰer]
  - [per] *sounds odd*
- Articulatory features that are not distinctive are called non-distinctive features. *Aspiration*
- Their presence is entirely predictable.

The Psychological Reality of Phonemes

- Native speakers of a language have no difficulty hearing one phoneme from another.
- Native speakers hear the configuration of the distinctive features and filter out the non-distinctive features.
- Non-distinctive features are perceived as only part of the accent.

Allophones

- Speakers do not utter phonemes.
- Phonemes are abstract representations of the sounds in a language that con-trast in the same environment.
- Allophones are the physical realizations of phonemes.
- Each phoneme must be realized by at least one allophone.

Phonemes capable in change the meaning

Allophones – what you actual pronouce

Allophones

- Each allophone of a phoneme is phonetically similar, yet distinct from all the others.
- Despite the phonetic difference, speakers recognize each as a representation of the same phoneme.

/X/

[x$_1$]   [x$_2$]   [x$_3$]

The Tree Metaphor

/tree/

[elm]   [pine]   [oak]   [palm]   [spruce]   [fir]   [willow]

Each particular example is a physical representation of the mental abstraction, "tree."
"Tree" exists as an abstract concept just as phoneme does.

Tree of trees
each allophone is a physical representation a phoneme tree

Allophones

- Unlike phonemes, allophones are described with a maximal amount of phonetic detail.
  - Whereas the phoneme /t/ is described as a voiceless alveolar stop, the allophone [tʰ] is described as a voiceless aspirated alveolar stop.

physical representation

Allophones

- Allophones do not contrast in the same environment.
  - Two allophones of the same phoneme can occur in the same environment without changing the meaning of the word.
  - This is called free variation.
  - Released and unreleased voiceless stops can occur in utterance final position.
    - stop [stap] [stap⁻]

phonemes
gust rust minimal pair contrast in same environment
norelease lips closed

Allophones

- Allophones are conditioned by phonological environment.
  - Aspiration in English
    - [pʰ] [tʰ] [kʰ] *voiceless stops*
    - The aspiration of voiceless stops occurs in absolute syllable initial position.
    - [pʰat] [spat]
    - [tʰon] [ston]
    - [kʰæt] [skæt]

different allophones in different places

Allophones

– Velarization of /l/.
- [l] is a voiced alveolar lateral which occurs before vowels.
  – [lɪft]   [last]
- [ɫ] is a voiced alveolar lateral with velar coarticulation; it occurs after vowels.
  – [ɛɫbo] [bɛɫ] [faɫ]

R

Allophones

– Vowels in open syllables are longer than those is closed syllables.
- [bo:]   [bot]
- [si:]   [sin]
- [be:]   [bet]
- [tu:]   [tun]

not lengthen

– endored syllabes ending consonant

lengthen
open
syllables
end
in vowel

Phonological Rules

- The behavior of allophones is predict-able and can be captured in rule.
  – Aspiration

voiceless stops became aspirated in absolute syllable position

$$\begin{bmatrix} - \text{voice} \\ - \text{cont} \\ - \text{del rel} \end{bmatrix} \longrightarrow [+\text{aspirated}] \ / \ . \underline{\quad}$$

   ↑   ↑   ↑

  input   output   environment

sound being made   *changed being in sound*

Phonological Rules

– Velarization of laterals ~~L~~

    [+ lateral] -----> [+ velar] / [+ vocalic] ___

    L becomes velarized after vowels

– Vowel lengthening

    [+ vocalic] -----> [+ long] / ____ .

    Vowel become lengthen when last sound in a syllable
    Vowels become lengthd in opened syllables

Complementary Distribution

- If allophones are induced by different environments, then allophones occur in distributional patterns.
  - The most frequent type of distribution is complementary distribution.
    - Each allophone of a phoneme appears in one and only one environment.
    - The environments are mutually exclusive.

Complementary Distribution

phoneme		/X/	
allophones	[x₁]	[x₂]	[x₃]
environments	A =/=	B =/=	C

Examples of Complementary Distribution

- The allophones of voiceless stops.
  - The aspirated allophones occur in syllable initial position and the unaspirated allophones occur everywhere else.
- The allophones of the lateral.
  - The velarized allophone occurs after vowels and the clear allophone occurs before vowels.

absolute syllable position

everywhere else

L after vowels

before vowels

in completely different environments

Assimilation

- One of the phonological processes that account for the complementary distri-bution of allophones is assimilation.
- In assimilation, a sound acquires a phonetic feature of a following sound.
  - Thus, different environments induce different allophones.

of allophone

normal dist.

when we speak normally a sound will acquire a phonetic feat. of following sound

complementary — the normal distributional patterns of allophones in the worlds languages

allophones of same phoneme occur in diff canological environ.

Discovering Assimilation

- Find a partner in the classroom; say the following pairs to each other; watch how the first sound is articulated.
  - twelve   tell
  - dwell   deli
  - quick   kick
  - shoe   she
  - juice   jest
  - sweet   seat

round   not rounded

words

u's & w's   assimilation   followed by round sum

Assimilation: Rounding

- twelve   [t̹]
- dwell   [d̹]
- quick   [k̹]
- shoe   [ʃ̹]
- goose   [g̹]
- sweet   [s̹]

- tell   [t]
- deli   [d]
- kick   [k]
- she   [ʃ]
- guess   [g]
- seat   [s]

Assimilation Rules

- In assimilation rules, the output is always the same as the environment.
- The input acquires a feature (the output) that is the same as the relevant feature in the environment.

- [+ cons] ----> [+ round] / _____ [+ round]

consonants become rounded before round sound

Assimilation: Dentalization

- In English an alveolar before a dental becomes dental.

– ten	[n]	tenth	[n̪]
– man	[n]	month	[n̪]
– well	[l]	wealth	[l̪]
– hell	[l]	health	[l̪]

- [+ alveolar] ----> [+ dental] / ___ [+ dental]

become   before

Assimilation: Nasalization

- In English, a vowel before a nasal becomes nasalized.
  - men [ĩ]   mit [ɪ]
  - tone [õ]   tote [o]
  - bum [ʌ̃]   bus [ʌ]
  - long [ã]   lot [a]

- [+ vowel] ----> [+ nasal] / ___ [+ nasal]

vowels before a nasal, vowels become nasalized ⟩ complimentary distribution

— not before a nasal, everywhere else

Practice

- Explain how assimilation produces sets of allophones that are in complementary distribution.

Assimilation always leads to complementary distributions

Output always same as the environment
Input acquires a feature

Assimilation
A sound acquires a phonetic feature of a following sound
so it can only acquires the feature if the following sound possesses it that feature

complementary
— different allophones of the same phoneme occur in mutually exclusive environments
2 sets of allophones that

Natural Classes

- A natural class can be described with fewer features than can any one sound in the class.
  - /t/ is a VL alveolar stop
  - /p/ /t/ /k/ are VL stops (a natural class)
  - /p/ /t/ /k/ /b/ /d/ /g/ are stops (a larger natural class).

Groups of sounds that somehow interact 2gether have phonetic feature

Natural Classes

- The concept of natural classes is important because phonological processes such as aspiration, rounding, nasalization, and dentalization apply to natural classes.
- The environments that trigger these phonological processes are also comprised of natural classes.

aspiration - vl stops
rounding - all consonants
nasalization - all vowels
dentalization - all alveolars

Natural Classes

- Some groups of sounds could never be identified as a natural class because they are too dissimilar in their configuration of articulatory features.
- /t/, /l/ and /m/ do not form a natural class because no configuration of features unites only those three sounds and excludes all others.

Practice

- Which groups of sounds below form a natural class.
  - /m/ /n/ /ŋ/ ✱ Class of nasals
  - /b/ /d/ /g/ /t/ 3 voiced stops and 1 voiceless stops
  - /f/ /s/ /θ/ /ʃ/ /h/ ✱ vl fricatives
  - /w/ /z/ /l/ /r/
  - /l/ /r/ /w/ /j/ ✱ non nasal consonants/the sonorants of english
  - /b/ /d/ /g/ ✱ voiced stops

Suprasegmentals

Beyond the Segmental Level

_____

_____

_____

_____

_____

_____

_____

What are Suprasegmentals?

- Those aspects of speech that involve more than single consonants or vowels.
- The features used to describe suprasegmentals are different from those used to describe segments: point of articulation, manner of articulation, and state of the glottis.

_____larger strength of language.____

_____

_____

_____

_____

_____

_____

What are Suprasegmentals?

- Suprasegmentals are contrastive because they can produce changes in meaning.
- There are 3 major suprasegmentals.
  - Stress *patterns*
  - Intonation
  - Tone *doesn't exist in engl*

_____rust dust_____

_____one sound changes the words_____

_____

_____

_____

_____

_____

Stress

- The characteristics of stress.
  - The use of extra respiratory energy during the production of a syllable.
    - Stress applies to entire syllables.
  - This extra respiratory energy moves more air out of the lungs meaning that stressed syllables are longer, louder, and higher in pitch.
  - Stress is contrastive.

change stress pattern you can change meaning

True in english

Word Stress Patterns

- Two strings of segments can be identical in their segmental composition, yet differ in meaning because they have different stress patterns.
  - verb   noun
  - [sʌbjɛkt]   [sʌbjɛkt]
  - [pɚmɪt] *permit*   [pɚmɪt] *permit*
  - [pɚvɚt]   [pɚvɚt] *pervert*
  - [kanflɪkt]   [kanflɪkt]
    conflict   *conflict*

verb stressed 2nd syllable   noun stressed 1st syllable

Grammatical Stress Patterns

- Two sequences may have the same words in them yet be different in meaning.
- Adjective and noun stress pattern.
  - In this pattern the noun receives primary stress.
    - [ə flæt fʊt] *A flatfoot*
    - [ə blu kot]
    - [ə blæk bord]

Grammatical Stress Patterns

- The compound stress pattern.
  - Compounds are two free morphemes that have been bound together to form a new word.
  - Compounds receive stress on the first element.
    - [ə flǽt fʊt]
    - [ə blú kot]
    - [ə blǽk bord]

Bring 2 words, put them together and stress the 1st one has an unique meaning *free*

Grammatical Stress Patterns

- Contrasts between the two patterns.
  - George bought a [blu bə́d]. *bird that happens to be blue*
  - George bought a [blu bə́d].
  - John found a [red kót] under Mary's bed.
  - John found a [rɛ́d kot] under Mary's bed.
  - Idiots usually live in the [wajt háws]. *a random house*
  - Idiots usually live in the [wájt haws]. *the actual white house*
- Grammatical stress is contrastive.

A Note on Compounds

- The meanings of adjective noun combinations are transparent if the speaker knows the meaning of both words:
  - a <u>hungry dog</u> is any dog that is hungry
  - an <u>interesting book</u> is any book that is interesting
  - a <u>remarkable story</u> is any story that is remarkable

no the meaning of adj. & nan y a no meaning, of the adj. combi

A Note on Compounds

- The meaning of a compound is not transparent.
  - a blackboard
  - a busybody
  - a house dog
  - a house cat
  - a dog house
  - a cat house

Practice

- Put the stress in the appropriate place.
  - Confederate soldiers were called [gré kots].
  - Don't write on the [blǽk bord].
  - Sally bought a [gre kót].
  - The Smiths bought the [grin háws] on the corner.
  - They grow tomatoes in their [grin haws].

Introduction to Intonation

- Listen to the following sentence. I will read it three times.
- Does the meaning change?
  - Bakersfield is a nice town.
  - Intonation pattern on all 3 sentences

simple declarative statement
question?
statement that has something following the sentence

What is Intonation?

- Intonation is the pitch contour over a phrase or sentence.
- Pitch is the rate of vibration of the vocal cords.
- Sounds with a higher pitch are produced with a greater frequency of vibration than are sounds with a lower pitch.

_____

_____

_____

_____

_____

_____

What is Intonation?

- Pitch is relative to the individual speaker.
- Pitch level is denoted with a number:
  - 2 is the speaker's normal pitch.
  - 1 is a level below normal or one that falls from the normal pitch.
  - 3 is a level above normal or one that rises from the normal pitch.

_____

_____

_____

_____

_____

_____

Pitch Contours are Contrastive

- As was demonstrated previously, pitch contours are contrastive.
- The same sequence of words take on different meanings if the pitch contour is changed.
  - Steve is a good student.
    - 231 falling stress
    - 233 rising stress pattern turn into a question
    - 232 qualifying statement after word

_____

_____

_____

_____

_____

_____

The Major Pitch Contours

- The major pitch contours are the 231. the 233, and the 232.
- The 231
  - The speaker starts the utterance with normal pitch. The pitch then rises to 3 over that word in the utterance which receives ⟨primary stress⟩ and then falls to 1.
  - In normal speech the 231 occurs with content questions, declarative statements and commands.

who, what, when, why

The day is monday

take out the book

The Major Pitch Contours

231

- Declarative statements
  - A university education is expensive.
  - "All my lust has turned to dust."
- Commands
  - Shut the door.
  - Take out your books.
- Content Questions
  - What is your name?
  - Who are you?

The Major Pitch Contours

- the 233
  - The speaker starts the utterance with normal pitch. The pitch then rises to 3 over that word in the utterance which receives primary stress and holds steady or actually rises a little more.
  - In normal speech the 233 occurs with ⟨yes/no⟩ questions.
    - Are you a student?
    - Is it raining?

The Major Pitch Contours

- the 232
  - To understand the 232 pattern, it is necessary to understand the concept of <u>tone group</u>: that part of a sentence over which a particular pitch contour extends. A short sentence may consist of a single tone group, but a longer sentence may have more than one.
  - The 232 pattern extends over initial phrases or clauses to indicate that more is to come.

indicates that a pause isn't being taken

The Major Pitch Contours

adverb clause , main clause

If I were you, I would study more.
2   32 2   3   1

declarative statement

By the way, the exam is quite easy.
2   32 2   31

John is smart (but)   *he or she may not utter right away*
2   32

short declarative statement

The Major Pitch Contours

- Though the 231, 232, and 233 pitch contours are normally associated with certain sentence types, remember that intonation can be used to create different meanings on the same sequence of words.
- The exam was long.
  - 231 233 232

associated w/ certain types of sentences, but can use them creatively as well

Practice

- Identify the 'normal' pitch contour of the utterances below:
  - Beethoven composed the 'Emperor Concerto.' 231
  - How many students were absent? 231
  - Did you like the movie? 203
  - Please open the window. 231
  - If you do well,... 232

Tone

- Most languages in the world are tone languages. There are over 1000 tone languages in Africa. Many Amerindian languages have tone as do Thai, Chinese, and Burmese.
- Tone refers to the pitch contour over strings of segments.
- How do tone and intonation differ?

Intonation pitch contour over strings of words not segment

Tone

- Tone is contrastive
- The same string of segments will have different meanings if stated with different tones.

Is not found in english

speakers changed total pattern over some things segments will change the meaning

Tone

- Examples from Thai:
  - naa   [_] low tone   "a nickname"
  - naa   [-] mid tone   "rice paddy"
  - naa   [⁻] high tone   "maternal uncle"
  - naa   [^] falling tone   "face"
  - naa   [v] rising tone   "thick"

Phonotactics

Permissible sound sequences in the language

study of how sound sequences are put together in different languages

What is Phonotactics?

- Phonotactics refers to the construction of permissible sequences of segments. *in a language*
- Just because a language has an inventory of segments, it does not mean that the segments can be combined in any manner.
- For example, English has both a /z/ and /b/, but not a single word in English begins with /zb/.

41 sounds in english

Examining Phonotactic Structures

- The best approach to study sequences of segments is to analyze the syllable structure of monosyllabic words.
- In this way, the structure of individual syllables can be analyzed without the influence of other syllables.

study words that consist one syllable

Syllable Structure

- The syllable consists of three constituents: the nucleus, the onset, and the coda.
- The nucleus.
  - The only mandatory constituent of a syllable.
  - The nucleus is the sonority peak of the syllable.
    - Sonority refers to the loudness of a sound when length, stress, and pitch are held constant.

no nucleus = no syllable

loudess sound in all language is a vowel

Syllable Structure

- Different classes of sounds have different degrees of sonority *liquid, glides, nasals*
  - vowels > consonantal sonorants > obstruents — *stops fricative, africaler*
- The nucleus of the syllable is generally a vowel as vowels are the most sonorant of all sounds.
- Sometimes a consonantal sonorant can be the nucleus of a syllable.

Syllable Structure

- These consonants that can be nuclei are called syllabic consonants.
  - rubble [rʌbl̩]
  - button [bʌtn̩]
- Only liquids and nasals can be syllabic consonants.
- They can only be syllabic consonants when they occur in unstressed syllables.

2 syllables in each word

Syllable Structure

- The onset.
  - An onset consists of all consonants before the nucleus in the same syllable.
  - The onset is less sonorant than the nucleus.
- The coda.
  - A coda consists of all consonants after the nucleus in the same syllable.
  - The coda is less sonorant than the nucleus.

The Universal Canonical Syllable Structure

- Syllables with both onsets and codas normally have a rise in sonority from the onset through the nucleus and a fall in sonority from the nucleus though the coda

nucleus

onset   coda

The UCSS

Vowel

glide   glide

liquid   liquid

nasal   nasal

obstruent   obstruent

sonority rising   falling sonority

onset   coda

breeze   salt

liquid   liquid obstruent

obstruent

english has violations of ucss

stop violates the ucss

Syllable Structure Conditions

- Syllable structure conditions define the permissible onsets and codas in a language.
- One-member onsets
  - One-member onsets can consist of all sounds in English except for /ŋ/. *1 consonant*
- Two-member onsets
  - There are two conditions for defining two-member onsets in English.

24 consonants в engl
/ŋ/ only occurs in coda position

Syllable Structure Conditions

Stop, Affricate, Fricative
  - An obstruent + a non-nasal consonantal sonorant.
    - black   flip   free
    - drip   trip   brick
  - /s/ + consonantal sonorant or another voiceless obstruent. *nasal liquid glide*
    - smoke   snow   slow *nasal*
    - stop   speak   skim *voiceless stop*
    - *sŋ-   *sr-

Syllable Structure Conditions

- Three-member onsets
  - /s/ + voiceless stop + non-nasal consonantal *liquid or slide* sonorant. *p t k*
  - Only eight of twelve possibilities occur.
    - street   /str/   split   /spl/
    - scream   /skr/   spring   /spr/
    - squeal   /skw/   spew   /spj/
    - skew   /skj/   sclerosis /skl/
- English does not have four-member onsets.

3 member onsets
longest onset in english

Syllable Structure Conditions

- One-member codas
  - All sounds can occur but /h/.
  - The rest of the syllable structure conditions for codas in English are so complicated that they will not be given.
  - English allows longer codas than onsets which is unusual for the world's languages.
  - English can have four-member codas.
    - twelfths /-lfθs/

Closed Syllables

- Though vowels are generally the nuclei of syllables, not all vowels can appear in every type of syllable.
- A closed syllable is one that has a coda, and any vowel in English can occur in a closed syllable.

  [hæt] [mɛt] [lɪd] [lat] [lʌk] [nid]
  [med] [lod] [krud] [hɚd] [wʊd]

Open Syllables

- Open syllables are those that do not have a coda.
  - A restricted number of vowels appear in stressed open syllables.
  - All tensed vowels including the diphthongs can appear in stressed open syllables.
  - Why do only certain vowels appear in stressed open syllables in English?

The Rhyme

- To understand the different distributions of vowels in closed and open syllables, it is necessary to introduce another constituent of the syllable, the rhyme.
- The rhyme is the nucleus and the coda taken as a unit. It stands in opposition to the onset.

Start coda — *short O*

the rhyme

The Rhyme

Syllable

Onset   Rhyme

Nucleus Coda

The Rhyme

- Sounds in all languages are associated with timing units. Nearly all consonants are associated with a single timing unit.
- However, some vowels—tense vowels and diphthongs—are clearly longer than others; they are associated with two timing units.

in english
Affricates — are two timing units
2 timing tensed vowel
beat bit - single timing
1 raxed vowel

Heavy Rhymes

- In English all stressed rhymes must be heavy; they must have at least two timing units.
- All closed syllables in English are automatically heavy because the rhyme must have both a nucleus and a coda as in the word bought.

short O coda
two timing units

Heavy Rhymes

                    Syllable
                   /   \
            Onset   Rhyme
              | /   \
              b   Nucleus   Coda
                         | |
                         a   t

- The rhyme in bought is heavy because the nucleus is comprised of one timing unit, and the coda is comprised of another timing unit.

Heavy Rhyme

long vowel

                    Syllable
                   /   \
            Onset   Rhyme
              | |
              b   Nucleus
                          /   \
                         i   i

- In contrast, the stressed mono-syllabic word bee is open. It does not have a coda, yet the rhyme is still heavy because the nucleus has a vowel that consists of two timing units.

Summary

- All stressed syllables in English must have heavy rhymes, those consisting of at least two timing units.
- Unstressed syllables may be 'light'; that is, they may consist of a single timing unit as in the words <u>the</u> and <u>a</u>.

Final Examples

- All the words in the right column below are impermissible because they are stressed open syllables that consist of a single timing unit.
  - /hi/   */hɪ/
  - /pe/   */pɛ/
  - /bu/   */bʊ/
  - /ro/   */rɔ/
- All rhymes are heavy in the words on the left.

Syllable Structure Conditions and Pronunciation

- Pronounce the following words:
  - Nkomo
  - Dmitri
  - Zgusta
  - Gdansk

  impermissible onset

- When speakers of a language are confronted by a syllable structure disallowed in their native language, they will modify it so that it conforms to acceptable syllable structure.

Syllable Structure Conditions and Pronunciation

- The most prevalent types of modification are deletion and epenthesis, the insertion of a reduced vowel.
- Most English speakers use epenthesis to separate the first two consonants on the words previously given Nkomo, Dmitri, Zgusta, Gdansk.

Syllable Structure Conditions and Pronunciation

- Even though all these underlined segments occur in English, the combinations do not.
- Native speakers of English modify the onsets because they violate the syllable structure conditions of the language.

English Spelling Patterns

The Correspondence between
Phonemes and Graphemes

close relationship w/
each phoneme &
grapheme.

The Alphabet

- The alphabet is a system of writing in which each written character is supposed to correspond to a distinctive sound in the language.
- The Greeks designed the first true alphabet around 800 B.C.E.
- The Romans borrowed the Greek alphabet and redesigned it to make it suitable for the writing of Latin.

Greek came up with the
1st true Alphabetic system

The Alphabet

- This Roman alphabet was finished about 100 C.E.
- English, even though it is a far different language from Latin, uses the Roman alphabet.

26 characters
40 phonemes

Graphemes

- Graphemes are written letters. of Alphanet
- Phonemes are the abstract representations of distinctive sounds in a language.
- The alphabet attempts to create a correspondence between graphemes and phonemes.
- No language has a one-to-one correspondence between its graphemes and phonemes.

Graphemes

- Some languages have a fairly close correspondence such as Spanish, Finnish and Italian.
  - gatto   gelato   spaghetti
  - cane   cera   chitarra
- In Italian, when <u>c</u> and g are before non-high front vowels they are pronounced as /k/ and /g/ as in <u>gatto</u> and <u>cane</u>.

Graphemes

- When <u>c</u> and g are before high front vowels, they are pronounced as affricates as in <u>gelato</u> and <u>cera</u>.
- The presence of <u>h</u> between either consonant and a following high front vowel blocks them from becoming affricates as in <u>spaghetti</u> and <u>chitarra</u>.

Graphemes

- Other languages such as French and English have a poor correspondence between phonemes and graphemes.
- English, for example, has approximately 41 phonemes, depending on dialect, but only 26 graphemes.
  - Consequently, problems of correspondence will occur.

Examples of the Lack of Correspondence

- Across words, one grapheme or group of graphemes can correspond to more than one phoneme.
  - Realizations of the letter c.
    - cello   /čɛlo/
    - cat   /kæt/
    - cyst   /sɪst/

Examples of the Lack of Correspondence

- Across words, one phoneme can correspond to more than one grapheme or combination of graphemes.
  - Spellings for /i/.
    - see   he   relieve
    - people   ravine   flea
    - receive   amoeba   Caesar
    - key   quay

11 different correspondence
to spelling /i/

71

Examples of the Lack of Correspondence

- Some graphemes do not have any phonemic correspondence.
  - bomb
  - knife
  - hymn
  - malign
  - sign
  - iamb

[handwritten: silent letter]

[handwritten: not pronounced]

How Irregular is English Spelling?

- As unsystematic as spelling in English may seem, many correspondences exist.
  - For example, all words pronounced with /θ/ or /ð/ will be spelled with a th.
  - However, not all words spelled with th are pronounced as /θ/ or /ð/.
    - Thai   Thailand
    - Thames   Thomas
    - thyme

How Irregular is English Spelling?

- The relationship between graphemes and phonemes representing consonants is fairly stable.
  - For example, a written f will usually be pronounced as /f/ though other combinations --gh and ph--may be pronounced as /f/ as well.
- There is more variation between graphemes and phonemes representing vowel sounds.

Spelling Patterns

- VC(C)#
- Pattern predicts a short vowel in <u>V</u> position.
  - bat   /bæt/   back   /bæk/
  - bet   /bɛt/   belt   /bɛlt/
  - bit   /bɪt/   list   /lɪst/
  - not   /nat/   lost   /last/
  - but   /bʌt/   lust   /lʌst/

short vowels

start at end of word then predict the vowel

Spelling Patterns

- There are exceptions to the VC(C) spelling pattern.
  - of
  - all
  - own
  - old

none of the predictions had due to none of the vowels are pronounced in short vowels

Spelling Patterns

- VCe#   *always ends in printed e*
- Pattern predicts a long vowel in <u>V</u> position.
  - rate   /ret/
  - Pete   /pit/
  - lice   /lajs/   *silent e*
  - poke   /pok/
  - rule   /rul/

long vowel quality

ignore the consonants before the printed vowel, they have nothing to do with how the vowel is pronounced

Spelling Patterns

- There are exceptions to the VCe# spelling pattern.
- The vowel in the V position may not be long.
  - have
  - love
  - give

vowels are not in long vowel quality

Spelling Patterns

- VV
- Pattern predicts the long vowel quality of the first printed <u>V</u>.
  - meat meet
  - receive
  - clue
  - fruit
  - straight
  - moat

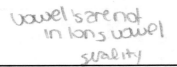

long vowel on first printed vowel

2 printed vowels have to be back to back

Spelling Patterns

- There are many exceptions to the VV spelling pattern.
- The long vowel quality may not be the quality of the first vowel.
  - freight   great   relieve
  - amoeba   too   youth
  - aisle   height   roof

the 2nd vowel is the long vowel pronounced

Spelling Patterns

- Another exception to the VV spelling pattern is that the vowel quality may be short.
  - bread   taut
  - guest   instead
  - enough   build
  - said   laugh

short vowel sound

Reasons for "Unphonemic" Spelling

- Languages evolve.
  - Language change, especially pronunciation, is normal.
  - One prominent example of a change in pronunciation was the Great Vowel Shift between 1400 and 1600.

vowels pronounced one way B4 1400 & pronounced differently after 1600

Shakespeare – modern early english   this english has evolved from what it is today

– great impact of spelling an pronunciation in english

Reasons for "Unphonemic" Spelling

Pre-Vowel Shift

/i/	/e/	/ɛ/	/u/
bite	beet	beat	foul
wise	freeze	please	house

/o/	/ɔ/	/a/
fool	rose	hate
goose	no	name

B4 great vowel shift, 1400

The final e was pronounced before, but now we no them as silent e's

Reasons for "Unphonemic" Spelling

- Conservative nature of spelling.
  - Even though pronunciation changes, spelling generally does not once it becomes standardized of the purposes of mass literacy.
  - Consequently, even if a language has a close phoneme-grapheme correspondence at one point in history, the correspondence may be much less evident later due to natural pronunci-ation changes and the immutability of spelling.
    - knight

Reasons for "Unphonemic" Spelling

spoken french

- The Normans conquered England in 1066.
- Over the next 200 years over 10,000 French words were incorporated into English including soldier, court, peasant, guard, traitor, govern, authority, prison, chancellor, arrest, judge, throne, nobility, lemon, grapes, and beef. *french words*

small sample of french words

Reasons for "Unphonemic" Spelling

- Not only did English incorporate French words into English, early scribes frequently used French-style spellings for words not borrowed from French:

cwen	→	queen
cwik	→	quick
cwellen	→	quell
scip	→	ship

these spellings were changed to match the french spellings later

spellings of the english words long ago

76

Reasons for "Unphonemic" Spelling

- Scribes also wrote words to show their etymological roots, especially words borrowed from Latin.
  - de**b**t   from   debitum
  - dou**b**t   from   dubium
  - pe**o**ple   from   populous
  - vi**c**tuals   from   victus

  } latin words

books were underlined letters and incorporated them in the english spellings

Standardizing English Spelling

- The invention of the printing press in the mid 15th century led to the standardization of the spelling of European languages.
- The first book in English was printed in 1485, and by the time of Shakespeare, the spelling of English had essentially been settled.

Standardizing English Spelling

- When the first books were being printed, the Great Vowel Shift was still occurring in English.
- Many of the spellings that attempted to capture the etymological roots of a word came into the standardized spelling system.
  - Consequently, standardized spelling in English does not really correspond closely to pronunciation.

Standardizing English Spelling

- The publication of Samuel Johnson's <u>A Dictionary of the English Language</u> in 1755 helped to further codify English spelling.
- However, the general public rejected some of Johnson's spelling: <u>musick</u>, <u>critick</u>, <u>attick</u>, <u>epick</u>, <u>publick</u>, <u>tropick</u>, and <u>chaotick</u>.
- Johnson had a general rule that a word could not end in a <u>c</u>.

Spelling Reform

Beware of heard, a dreadful word
That looks like beard and sounds like bird
and dead; it's said like bed, not bead;
For goodness sake, don't call it deed!
Watch out for meat and great and threat
(They rhyme with suite and straight and debt).
A moth is not a moth in Mother,
Nor both in bother, broth in brother.
         (Richard Krogh).

Spelling Reform

- Since the 1700s, some very influential scholars have advocated reform of the English spelling system.
- Would be spellraisers include Benjamin Franklin, Noah Webster, Mark Twain, and George Bernard Shaw.

Spelling Reform

- George Bernard Shaw is noted for asserting that fish could be spelled as ghoti.
  - /f/ as in enough *represents f sound*
  - /ɪ/ as in women *short i sound*
  - /ʃ/ as in nation *ti sh sound*
- Mark Twain asserted that English spelling was "invented by a drunken thief."

Noah Webster

- Noah Webster published two American dictionaries in 1806 and 1828. In them he included some spellings that were different from those found in Johnson's British dictionary
- Webster wanted to simplify some spelling.
- More importantly he wanted to differentiate American spelling from British spelling.

① simplify some spellings
② differenate from American spelling from british spelling since we just fought the war against the British, 1812

Johnson and Webster

British   *American*

plough	plow
almanack	almanac
publick	public
humour	humor
goal	jail
centre	center
theatre	theater
offence	offense

Current Situation

- Even today thousands of words in English have more than one spelling: blond/blonde, grey/gray, disk/disc, leaped/leapt, woolen/woollen, and cauldron/caldron.
- Even though compounds are one word, they are sometimes written as if they were two: lightning rod and the White House.

Why Spelling Reform Would Not Work

- The whole corpus of writings in English would have to be changed.
- English pronunciation would continue to change even after spelling was reformed.
- It would be difficult to select the English dialect on which to base the spelling reform.
- Current spelling is associated with "being educated."

More is printed in english than any other language

- english would continue to change

Why Spelling Reform Would Not Work

- Morphological relationships among words would be lost.
  - hymn — hymnal
  - damn — damnation
  - malign — malignant
  - resign — resignation
  - sign — signature
  - bomb — bombard
  - iamb — iambic

When you add another morpheme to the word the silent letters reappear

Ind ov speling patrnz

Lectures
in
Morphology
and
Word Classes

Morphology

Creating the Words of a Language

how words are put together & how they are pronounced

Morphology Defined

- The component of grammar that deals with the internal structure of words.
- Morphology consists of morphemes, rules for combining them into words, and rules for pronouncing the resulting words.
- Knowledge of morphology allows speakers to correctly form words, interpret new words, and pronounce words.

sub units - morphemes

Some Examples

- Blick is a nonsense word.
  - What does re-blick mean? *again*
  - What is the word class of re-blick? *past tensed form - verb*
  - What is the word class of blick? *blick has to be a verb*
- Groosh is another nonsense word.
  - What does groosh-able mean? *ab*
  - What is the word class of groosh-able? *adjectives*
  - What is the word class of groosh? *verbs*

Re = again
only verbs has past tense

able to read
able - to be capable
able binds to only verbs
so that means groosh

able creates adj

Morpheme Defined

- A morpheme is the minimal unit of meaning or grammatical function in a language.
  → {book} {from} {of} grammatical function *meaning*
- A morpheme may be a word or less than a word.
  – {course} {re-} {-ment}
- A morpheme cannot be divided into smaller meaningful units.

you cant divide the morpheme into subdivision

Bind together to create words

book - version, word

from - has an actual definits

-ment - derives noun from adj

Morpheme Defined

- Examine the following words: *not* *not* *not*
  – uninteresting uneventful unlivable
- What does {un-} mean in those words?
- Does {un-} mean the same thing in the following words? doesn't mean not
  – untie undress untangle *reverse the process*
- Try to define {un-} as used above.

reverse the process

2 un's 2 different morphemes of un

Morpheme Defined

- Even though two morphemes are pronounced the same, they are distinct morphemes if their meanings are different.
- What does {un-} mean in the following words?
  – unloosen unearth unnerve
- In these examples {un-} is not a distinct morpheme, but an inherent part of the word.

un = means nothing
inherent part of the word

unloosen – doesn't mean anything, don't need the un not a seperate morpheme w/ a distinct meaning

The Concept of Word

- A word is a minimal free form in a language.
  - A free form can stand on its own.
    - What are those?
    - Houses.
  - Houses is a free form.

↑ able to stand on its own

plural morpheme is not a
free form can't stand on
its own to answer question
(es)

Simple Words

- Simple words are free forms that consist of only one morpheme. *monomorphemic words*
- Most function words in English are simple words.
  - Prepositions: in at on for from *function words*
  - determiners: a an the this
  - conjunctions: and but or because } - function words
  - degree adverbs: very so quite too

monomorphemic words - any word that consist of a single morpheme is a simple word

simple words in morphology
isn't that much interest

Complex Words

- Complex words consist of more than one morpheme.
  - quickness = {quick} {-ness} 2 morphemes
  - runners = {run} {-er} {-s} 3 morphemes
  - undeniably = {un-} {deny} {able} {ly} 4 morphemes
- Morphology is much more concerned with complex words than with simple words.

Practice

- Find the morphemes in the words below.
  - artichoke *single morpheme arti isn't separate*
  - establishments *3*
  - shrewish *2*
  - creativity *3*
  - unfriendly *3*
    not friend ly

Types of Morphemes

- Free morphemes
  - A free morpheme can stand on its own.
  - It has a self contained meaning independent of that of all other morphemes.
  - All simple words are free morphemes.

All monomorphemic words are free morphemes

Bound Morphemes

- A bound morpheme cannot stand on its own.
- Its inherent meaning is manifest only when it is attached to another morpheme.
  - {-er} *can't stand on its own*
  - {-ly}   *does mean something when bound to something*

nouns

adverbs - adjectives

Roots

- A root is that morpheme which carries the principal meaning in a word.
  - cats: cat is the root
  - childish: child is the root
- It is also that part of a word that remains after all affixes have been removed.
- Most roots in English are free morphemes.

Bases

- Bases are morphological structures to which affixes may be bound.
- Bases may consist of more than one morpheme.
- All roots are also bases, but not all bases are roots.
  - can add affixes to roots

judgements
judgement - Base
judge - root

Bases

- Examine the following set of words:
  - child
  root - childish 2 morphemes
  root - childishly
- Child is both the root and base of childish.
- Childish is the base of childishly, but child is still the root.

childish - Base
child is still the root

Bases

- English has a word based morphology:
  - Words are built from other free forms. Free forms that are bases are free bases.
- Bound morphemes that are bases are bound bases. *not a freeform*
  - dental: dent is a bound base
- A bound base must have at least one affix attached to it to form a legitimate word.

dental

not all bases are free bases

- freeforms serve as
the bases for new words
childishly
freeform

Affixes

- An affix is a bound morpheme that must be attached to a base.
- Affixes may be described by their position relative to the base:
  - prefix suffix infix — *into a base* *after*
- Affixes may be described by their function.
  - inflectional morpheme
  - derivational morpheme

always bound

Affixes by Position: Prefixes

- Prefixes occur before the base.
- English has approximately 75 prefixes
  - {extra-} {marital}
  - {dis-} {enchanted}
  - {re-} {think}
  - {ex-} {spouse}
- Normally, only one prefix is bound to the base.

there's exceptions
the un is normally the one *not*

Affixes by Position: Prefixes

- A few words may have more then one prefix.
  - {suppose}
  - {pre suppos ing}
  - {un pre suppos ing}
- English prefixes are additive not replacive. They are simply added on to the base.

add prefixes

In general engl doesn't
Pusp on words (prefixs)

Affixes by Position: Suffixes

- Suffixes occur after the base.
- A base may take up to four suffixes.
  - norm
  - norm al
  - norm al ize
  - norm al ize r
  - norm al ize r s
- Suffixes in English are also additive.

not repracesive

pefers adding suffixes to
words instead of profixer

Affixes by Position: Infixes

- An infix occurs within a base.
- Infixes occur in languages such as Bontoc and Tagalog spoken in the Philippines
- Example from Tagalog.
  - takbuh "run"   tumakbuh "ran" *past tense*
  - lakad "walk"   lumakad "walked" *past tense*
- What is the infix? *um*
- Where does it occur? *1st consant of the vowels*

english doesn't have
infixes

Affixes by Position: Infixes

- In languages that have infixes, they are quite regular and productive.
- Does English have infixes?
  - man men (goose geese) foot feet
- The changes above are irregularities in the language and not cases of the use of productive infixes.

the changes have no relation

vowel
high back   high front   vowel

*this would be an example
of replacsive infixer since
it replaces letters to the
words — doesn't make
sense in Engl*

Affixes by Function: *grammatical function*
Derivational Affixes

- Derivational affixes can derive a word whose word class is different from that of the base.
  - {pain} (n) + {-ful} = painful (adj)
  - The derivational affix {-ful} derives adjectives from nouns.

Affixes by Function:
Derivational Affixes

- Derivational affixes can also derive words whose meaning is quite different from that of the base.   *derivational affix*
  - {brother} (n) + {-hood} = brotherhood (n)
  - The word brother means male sibling, but brotherhood has nothing to do with male siblings.

*cuz brother &
brotherhood means
something completely different*

hood derivational affix

Affixes by Function: Derivational Affixes

- Derivational affixes generally apply to only a small subset of bases in a word class.
  - verb   {-ment}
  - judge   judgment
  - curtail   curtailment
  - establish   establishment
  - speak   *speakment
  - believe   *believement

Derives nouns

derive from -?
small group of bases in a particular word class

ment Binds to verbs to form noun

can't derive those words to become a noun

Affixes by Function: Derivational Affixes

- Derivational affixes carry semantic, not grammatical, content.
  - They create words with new meanings.
    - {pre-} determine
    - {un-} successful
    - {sub-} standard
    - {ex-} lawyer

- derive words that mean something quite different

Affixes by Function: Derivational Affixes

- Derivational affixes may be prefixes or suffixes.
  - {pre-} nominate   involve {-ment}
  - {sub-} normal   sorrow {-ful}
  - {ex-} general   rapid {-ly}
  - {re-} invent   electric {-ity}
  - {un-} happy   happy {-ness}

Affixes by Function: Derivational Affixes

- Generally, derivational affixes that are prefixes do not derive a word whose class is different from that of the base.

verb – {pre-} nominate verb
adj – {sub-} normal adj
noun – {ex-} felon noun
verb – {re-} invent verb
adj – {un-} happy adj

Affixes by Function: Derivational Affixes

- Generally, derivational affixes that are suffixes derive a word whose class is different from that of the base.

verb involve {-ment} noun
noun – sorrow {-ful} adj
adj – rapid {-ly} adv
adj – electric {-ity} noun
adj – happy {-ness} noun

Practice

- Identify the word class of each base in the words below and the word class of the derived word.

verb – active adj   verb preregister verb
noun – manly adj   verb swimmer noun
adj – happiness noun   logical adj
adj – impossible adj   verb readable adj

Affixes by Function: Inflectional Affixes

- English has **eight inflectional affixes** that co-occur with words of particular classes.
- Two inflectional morphemes co-occur with nouns.
  - the plural *1st* noun *s*
    - book books   table tables
  - the possessive *2nd*
    - Tom Tom's   the man   the man's *'s*

Affixes by Function: Inflectional Affixes

- **Four inflectional affixes co-occur with verbs.**
  - 3rd person singular of the present tense
    - run runs
    - speak speaks   *Present tense & subject can be replaced by he she or it*
  - past tense   *s w/ He she or it*
    - walk walked *ed*
    - cook cooked

Affixes by Function: Inflectional Affixes

- past participle   *the diffee between past tense & past participle*
  - repair repaired   *used w/ cert auxiliary verbs*
  - kill killed
- present participle
  - swim swimming
  - read reading   *ing*

Affixes by Function:
Inflectional Affixes

- Two inflectional affixes co-occur with gradable adjectives.
  - comparative
    - big bigger
    - smart smarter   *er*
  - superlative
    - big biggest
    - smart smartest   *est*

Affixes by Function:
Inflectional Affixes

- Inflectional affixes do not change the word class of the <u>stem</u> that they are bound to.
  - They bind to stems of given word classes and the resulting word is of the same word class.
- A stem is essentially a word to which all desired morphological word building processes have applied other than inflectional affixing.

Characteristic

Affixes by Function:
Inflectional Affixes

- In English, all inflectional affixes are suffixes.
- Only one inflectional affix occurs on a stem.
- They always occur last.
- They are productive in that they apply to nearly all stems in a given word class.

Ex) All count nouns can be pluralized using the plural morpheme

Affixes by Function: Inflectional Affixes

- However, some stems are irregular and do not take the regular inflectional morphemes.
  - Suppletion is one type of irregularity. A form in a grammatical paradigm has no resemblance to the base form.
    - walk walks walking walked *related to one another*
    - go goes going (went) *suppletive form no way of being, its related to the other words*
  - Went is a suppletive form for the past tense of go.

Affixes by Function: Inflectional Affixes

- A second type of irregularity is the use of ablaut, the replacement of one vowel for another to express an inflectional contrast.
- In English ablaut especially occurs in irregular verbs in the past tense:
  - [brek]   [brok]   *break breaked not real*
  - [spik]   [spok]
  - [lid]   [lɛd]

irregularities

different vowel quality than each

Regular and Irregular Stems

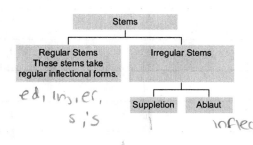

ed, ing, er, s, 's

inflection change occurs

97

Affixes by Function: Inflectional Affixes

- The last feature of inflectional morphemes is that they carry grammatical, not semantic, content
  - Grammatical information relates certain words in sentences to one another.
    - Nigel speaks Zulu.
  - The [-s] on the verb merely acts as an agreement marker with the subject. It has no real semantic content.

If you take out the S on speaks It still means the same

Deletion of Inflectional Morphemes

- Because inflectional morphemes carry redundant information, speakers learning English as a second language sometimes delete them in their speech.
- English speaking children and non-native English speaking children will also variably delete them in their writing.

Deletion of Inflectional Morphemes

- Research in the writing of elementary school students reveals that as the students get older they delete a smaller percentage of inflectional morphemes. In one study fourth graders deleted 7.9% of inflectional morphemes and sixth graders deleted 6.4%.

Deletion of Inflectional Morphmemes

- Non-native English speaking students delete a greater percentage of inflectional morphemes than do native English speaking students.
- However, the same pattern for age holds constant. As students get older, they delete a smaller percentage of inflectional morphemes.

Deletion of Inflectional Morphemes

- On the following slide is a short essay written by a native Spanish-speaking fourth grader.
- Just do not note the number of deletions; pay close attention that their absence can be accounted for because they carry redundant information supplied by the context of the written passage.

Student Essay

- the kangaroo was jumping the fence because he was seein how much he can jump and he jump 16 feet high and then he jump again and he was gled that he could jump that high because he think wasin cana jump 16 feet high from the fence and he almoset Fall down because he didn't know ther was a fance and then he saw there

Student Essay

- was'nt no more time and he jump so high that nobody though that was a kangaroo and he almos canat fall on the Tree but he jump the tree but he did't touch a little leave and he did'nt care have he broke his leg or hang but only what he whant to do is chest to jump high and he like to jump because he was a kangaroo.

put comments about this essay in BBunder morphology

Reasons for the Deletion of Inflectional Morphemes

- Young students variably delete inflectional morphemes because they are concentrating on the content of their writing and not on form.
- They also delete inflectional morphemes because the morphemes are weak in semantic content and carry redundant information.

Reasons for the Deletion of Inflectional Morphemes

- Note that young students almost never delete derivational morphemes. This is due to the strong semantic content carried by derivational morphemes.
- If students drop the <u>un-</u> from <u>unpopular</u>, they will completely change the meaning of what they were trying to write.

Misconceptions about Deletion

- Some teachers believe that students do not understand the past tense because they occasionally delete the past tense morpheme.
- Such a belief is completely inaccurate. Children frequently use adverbials when writing in the past tense, showing that they understand time before the present.

yesterday last week nearly showing time before the present

Misconceptions about Deletion

- If children did not understand the past tense, then they should sometimes use past tense morphemes when writing in the present tense. This almost never happens.
- In addition, when writing in the past tense, children usually write the past tense forms of irregular verbs correctly, indicating that the problem is with the regular inflection.

Dealing with the Deletion of Inflectional Morphemes

- As children grow older they naturally delete a smaller percentage of inflectional morphemes. Consequently, teachers do not have to mark students' papers with red ink.
- Usually if a teacher asks students to read a sentence out loud, the students pronounce the deleted morpheme and can then write it on the paper.

The Regularity of Word Structure

- The structure of complex words is quite regular and can be captured in trees.
- Use <u>impossibility</u> as an example. The root is <u>possible</u>, but it has two bound morphemes, {im-} and {–ity}. One must bind to the root before the other.
- How can you decide?

The Regularity of Word Structure

- <u>Possible</u> is an adjective. The prefix {im-} binds to adjectives, but the suffix {–ity} also binds to adjectives.
- {im-} derives an adjective from an adjective, and {–ity} derives a noun from an adjective; {im-} must bind to the root first because {im-} cannot bind to a noun, which would be the case if {-ity} binds first.

The Regularity of Word Structure

- This order can be seen in the tree on the right.
- {im-} binds to <u>possible</u> first, forming the adjective <u>impossible</u>.
- {-ity} then binds to <u>impossible</u>, forming the noun <u>impossibility</u>.

The Pronunciation of Morphemes

- Morphemes are abstractions just as phonemes are.
- Allomorphs are the physical realizations of morphemes.
- Each morpheme must have one or more allomorphs.
- Allomorphs appear in square brackets [].

— speakers don't pronounce morphemes
— allomorphs are what is spoke

The Pronunciation of Morphemes

- Many affixes in English have a single allomorph.
  - The {-ly} suffix that derives adverbs from adjectives is always pronounced as [li].
  - The comparative and superlative morphemes also have a single allomorph each.

bigger biggest

Allomorphy

- If a morpheme has two or more allomorphs, it is possible to study their distribution.
- The presence of each allomorph is triggered by a different phonological environment.
- If a prefix has more than one allomorph, the relevant environment will likely be the first sound of the base to which it is bound.

Allomorphy

- If a suffix has more than one allomorph, the relevant environment will likely be the last sound of the base to which it is bound.
- The different allomorphs of a given morpheme are usually in complementary distribution.

Example of Allomorphy

- English has a prefix {ɪn-}, meaning <u>not</u>, which binds to some adjectives.
- The first sound of the adjective determines which allomorph will occur.
- This variation is especially evident before adjectives beginning with an obstruent.
  - The nasal in the prefix becomes homorganic with the first obstruent sound of the adjective.

Example of Allomorphy

Example words with the prefix {ɪn-}.	Place of articulation of the nasal in the prefix
• impossible	• bilabial
• intolerant	• alveolar
• incoherent	• velar (<u>c</u> pronounced as [k]).
• infirm	• labiodental

Morphophonemic Rules

- The regularities that you have just discovered can be captured in rule.
- Rules that account for alternations among allomorphs are called morphophonemic rules.
- How morphemes are combined and pronounced depends on both morphology and phonology.

— past tense morphemes

— final sound of the verb ⟶ regular
will determine what sound
will be pronounce
(phonology)

Morphophonemic Rules

- Morphophonemic rules take into account that certain morphemes co-occur with each other. For example, the {ɪn-} morpheme only co-occurs with certain adjectives.
- The allomorphs are phonologically conditioned because the first sound of the adjective determines which allomorph will be bound to it.

, morpheme
im_possible

Morphophonemic Rules

- To capture the behavior of {ɪn-}, a nasal assimilation rule in required
- Before constructing this rule, we need to determine the base allomorph, the one from which the others will be derived.
- In the case of {ɪn-} the base nasal is [n] because it appears before all vowels as in inoperable and ineffective.

Morphophonemic Rules

- An informal form of the rule would essentially state that the alveolar nasal in the [ɪn-] allomorph of {ɪn-} assimilates to the point of articulation of the first sound of the adjective to which it is bound provided that the sound is an obstruent.
  - The situation is actually more complicated as evidenced in the words <u>illegible</u> and <u>irregular</u>.

Suffixal Homophones

- The plural, possessive, and the third person singular of the present tense all have sets of allomorphs which sound identical to one another and which are triggered by the same phonological environments.
- Why don't speakers of English confuse these different morphemes if they all sound the same?

syntactic & morphophical

- plural binds to regular
count nouns & only count
nouns
- possive binds to nouns a
becomes possive boy's
books now it occups what
a dj in engl

Form Classes

Word Classes that Can Be Identified
by Their Morphological Form

Defining Form Classes

- Membership in one of these classes is determined by the forms of the words.
- The class can be identified by the presence of derivational or inflectional morphemes that constitute the word.
- Word classes that can be identified by their derivational form are nouns, verbs, adjectives, and adverbs.

morphicolgical constructions

4 Big form classes of english

Defining Form Classes

- Word classes that can be identified by their inflectional form include nouns, gradable adjectives, and verbs.
  - Inflectional form can be actual or potential.
- The word classes that constitute the form classes are open classes
  - They admit new membership.

Books plural morph.
Book noun
inflectionze morpheme

Eng invents new nouns, words, and Bammaw too

Nouns and Derivational Morphemes

- Some derivational morphemes derive nouns and only nouns from bases of different word classes.
- Remember that derivational morphemes are generally not highly productive and will apply to only a few bases in a given class.

inflectional morphemes are much more useful to discover class than derivational

Nouns and Derivational Morphemes

Word Class of Base	Base	Derivational Morpheme	Derived Word
Verb	establish	-ment	establishment
Adjective	capable	-ity	capability
Adjective	fair	-ness	fairness

-ment drives nouns from verb

<u>Nouns</u> and Inflectional Morphemes: The Plural

- To say that nouns can be pluralized is too strong of a statement.
- English has sub-classes of nouns.
- – <mark>Proper nouns</mark> are usually capitalized, and generally cannot be modified by determiners or pluralized.
  - Mississippi
  - New York City
  - Son of Sam

Proper nouns are subcategories of nouns.

Nouns and Inflectional Morphemes:
The Plural

2nd

<u>Mass nouns</u> (non-count nouns) cannot be pluralized.
- linguistics   haste   tennis   sugar   water
— They cannot be modified with numerals:
- *two wine
— They can be modified by indefinite quantifying determiners such as <u>some</u>, <u>any</u>, and <u>enough:</u>
- some milk   enough wine   any sugar

Nouns and Inflectional Morphemes:
The Plural

3rd

— The most common sub-class of noun is the <u>count noun</u>, perhaps as many as 85% of all nouns in English.
— These nouns can be pluralized.
- course (s) book(s) pencil(s) noun(s) desk(s)
— These nouns can be modified by numerals and quantifying determiners that express the potential of being counted..
- two books   several courses   many nouns

Types of Nouns in English

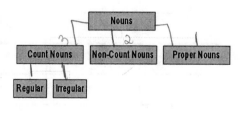

Man – Men
Woman – Women
Ox – Oxen

Nouns and Inflectional Morphemes: The Plural

- Almost all count nouns in English are regular and can be pluralized with the regular plural inflectional morpheme.
  - computer   computers
  - house   houses
  - stick   sticks
- Some count nouns are exceptional, for even though they can be made plural, the form is irregular.

Nouns and Inflectional Morphemes: The Plural

- Exceptional count nouns:
  - goose   geese
  - foot   feet
  - man   men
  - woman   women
  - ox   oxen
  - child   children

Nouns and Inflectional Morphemes: The Plural

- Other count nouns do not change form for the plural.
- Examples of count nouns that do not change form:
  - sheep   sheep
  - deer   deer
  - fish   fish

count nouns b/c we can put numerals in-front of them

Nouns and Inflectional Morphemes: The Plural

- Even though some irregular count nouns are evident in English, they are still count nouns because they can be modified by numerals and quantifying determiners:
  - two sheep
  - several geese
  - some children
  - a lot of fish

Count Nouns and the Plural

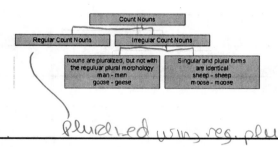

plurared using reg. plural morphemes as in dog : dogs
horse : horses

Nouns and Inflectional Morphemes: The Possessive

- As is true of all inflectional morphemes. the possessive appears to co-occur with the words of a single word class--in this case, nouns.
  - Mary's class   the fox's tail
- However, the possessive can bind to entire noun phrases:
  - the Queen of England's crown

Bound to entire noun phrase not just Queen

Nouns and Inflectional Morphemes: The Possessive

- Unlike other inflectional morphemes, the possessive appears to derive a word of a different word class--a determiner.
  - Tom's job is not very satisfying.
  - His job is not very satisfying.
- In the example above his substitutes for Tom's. Because his is a determiner , then Tom's must also be a determiner.

Nouns and Inflectional Morphemes: The Possessive

- The possessive can also function as a complete noun phrase in itself, actually a type of noun phrase substitute, a proform.
  - Tom's job is not very satisfying.
  - But John's is.
- In this example, John's substitutes for the entire noun phrase, Tom's job.

- that means John's is a type of proform

Singular and Plural Possessive

- In oral English, the singular and plural possessive sound identical.
- Some sentences taken out of context could be ambiguous.
  - The dogs food ran out (apostrophe omitted).
  - Is this one dog or more?

Singular and Plural Possessive

- In written English, however, the ambiguity is resolved by the different placement of the apostrophe.
  - The dog's food ran out. *1 dog*
  - The dogs' food ran out. *more than one dog*
- You have all heard a rule for the placement of apostrophes in English.
- What is the rule?

If a word ends in an s put an apostrophe

Singular and Plural Possessive

- Make the following words possessive.
  - Tess
  - Roger
  - cats
  - ox
  - oxen
  - Charles
  - doctors

Using the Apostrophe in Written English

Stem	Plural	Singular Possessive	Plural Possessive
child	children	child's	children's
teacher	teachers	teacher's	teachers'
Thomas	Thomases	Thomas's	Thomases'

Singular and Plural Possessive

- Reformulate the rule. Work together.
- If the written noun ends in the -s of plurality, form the possessive with an apostrophe after the -s. In all other cases, use 's to form the possessive.

Rule

Verbs and Derivational Morphemes

- A small number of derivational suffixes derive verbs from bases of other word classes.
- The newly derived verbs are all regular.

Verbs and Derivational Morphemes

Word class of base	Base	Derivational morpheme	Derived word
noun	length	-en	lengthen
adjective	ripe	-en	ripen
adjective	solid	-ify	solidify
noun	beauty	-ify	beautify

Verbs and Inflectional Morphemes

- English has four inflectional morphemes that co-occur with verb stems.
  - The third person singular of the present tense.
  - The past tense *-ed*
  - The progressive participle *-ing present*
  - The perfect/passive participle *have walked past*
- The two most regular forms are the present tense and the progressive participle.

He walks

present
3rd person } regular

past tense } irregular
speak

I walk

we walk

He/she walks

Regular Verbs

- Most verbs in English are regular and will have at least four distinct forms:
  - *stem* walk *3rd* walks *past* walked *present* walking *past participle* walked
  - visit visits visited visiting visited
- The past tense and perfect/passive *Past* participle forms of regular verbs are written and pronounced identically in English.

I walked yesterday
I have walked

Irregular Verbs

- For a verb to be irregular in English only one form in the paradigm needs to be irregular.
  - speaks spoke speaking spoken
  - chooses chose choosing chosen
  - cuts cut cutting cut
- The irregular forms are almost always the past tense and perfect/passive participle. *Past*

Reg forms tend to be
Past tense/past participe

Past tense + past particle
tend to be diff from each
other

Tests for Finding Verbs

- Main verbs in the present and past tense change form for changes in tense. This is true of both regular and irregular verbs.
- On the next slide are several sentences in the present tense; put the word <u>yesterday</u> in front of each sentence and state them again. The verb is the word that changes form when the word <u>yesterday</u> is added.

Tests for Finding Verbs

yesterday

- – John <u>writes</u> his papers on a typewriter.
- – The dogs <u>eat</u> their food greedily.
- – The newspaper <u>arrives</u> early in the morning.
- – A strong wind <u>blows</u> from the east.
- – The sautéed asparagus <u>is</u> good.
- This technique works well with children and allows them to find many verbs.

the verbs change
when putting yesterday
infront of the sentence

Adjectives and
Derivational Morphemes

- Some derivational suffixes derive adjectives from bases of other word classes.

Adjectives and Derivational Morphemes

Word class of base	Base	Derivational morpheme	Derived word
noun	poison	-ous	poisonous
noun	nation	-al	national
noun	king	-ly	kingly
verb	assert	-ive	assertive

More on Suffixal Homophones

- Many of you have heard that if a word ends in -<u>ly</u>, it is an adverb. Examine the words below to determine the word class of the base and the derived word.
  - friend   friendly
  - dead   deadly
  - quick   quickly

Adjectives and Inflectional Morphemes

- The two inflectional morphemes that co-occur with adjectives are the comparative and the superlative.
- However, they do not apply to all adjectives, but rather to a sub-class called gradable adjectives.
- Make the words below comparative and superlative.
  - fat thin smart happy crazy

fat fatter fattest

gradu ? dule adj

thin thinnest thinner

Adjectives and Inflectional Morphemes

- Now try to make these words comparative and superlative.
  - dead pregnant alive lost last first
- These words are non-gradable adjectives.
- What is the difference between the two types of adjectives?

Adjectives and Inflectional Morphemes

light on/off

- The semantic quality expressed by a non-gradable adjective is either extant or not.
- In contrast, the semantic quality expressed by a gradable adjective has many different degrees of realization. *many different positions*

tall taller tallest

a light switch

dead or not dead
present or not present

Adjectives and Inflectional Morphemes

- Other adjectives appear to be gradable, but they cannot be made comparative or super-lative through the use of inflectional morphemes.
  - beautiful
  - intelligent
  - interesting
- Are these adjectives gradable?
- Can they be comparative and superlative?

Adjectives and Inflectional Morphemes

- These words can be made comparative and superlative through the use of the words more and most.
  - more beautiful   most beautiful
  - more intelligent   most intelligent
  - more interesting   most interesting

Gradable adj, can't use the normal rules they use the word more & most

Adjectives and Inflectional Morphemes

- By examining the gradable adjectives below, discover the regularity for why some are formed into the comparative and the superlative morphologically whereas others are formed syntactically. *syllable structure*
  - tall   statuesque
  - pretty   beautiful
  - smart   intelligent
  - great   stupendous

** not based on semantic characteristics **

Other Ways to Test for Adjectives

- As you have seen only a few morphemes exist for deriving adjectives from bases of other word classes.
- Fortunately, a very simple test exists for distinguishing adjectives from other word classes.
- You can test for adjectives by using an adjective frame.

The Adjective Frame

- Only words of certain classes can fill a particular syntactic position.
- One such position is between a determiner and a noun.
- Any one word that appears between a determiner and a noun is an adjective.

The Adjective Frame

Test

Determiner

- the
- this
- a   _____
- an
- that

- book
- house
- student
- idea
- water

Adverbs and Derivational Morphemes

- Adverbs are harder than the other form classes to recognize by their morphological structure.
- No inflectional morphemes apply to adverb stems.
- Few derivational morphemes derive adverbs from bases of other word classes.
- A large number of adverbs do not have any special morphological features.

Adverbs and Derivational Morphemes

Word class of base	Base	Derivational morpheme	Derived word
adjective	quick	-ly	quickly
noun	health	-wise	healthwise
noun	sky	-ward	skyward

general adverbs

General Adverbs

- General adverbs are those that end in the derivational morpheme {-ly}, which can bind to both gradable and non-gradable adjectives.
  - quick → quickly
  - absolute → absolutely

44

Tests for Finding Adverbs

- Because so few derivational morphemes derive adverbs from bases of other word classes, very few morphological clues are available for distinguishing adverbs from words of other word classes.
- However, adverbs are very mobile in English and can easily be moved from one position to another.

Moving Adverbs

- Sentence Adverbs
  - It rained for forty days <u>unfortunately</u>.
  - <u>Unfortunately</u>, it rained for forty days.
- Predicate Adverbs
  - The Germans were <u>decisively</u> defeated at the Battle of the Bulge.
  - The Germans were defeated <u>decisively</u> at the Battle of the Bulge.

Structure Classes

Words that Establish Structural Relationships between Words in the Form Classes

Features of Structure Classes

- Structure classes are closed classes.
  - They have a limited membership.
  - New members are not readily admitted.
- Structure classes are not recognized by form, but rather by position.
  - The words of each class occur in a fixed position relative to the words in another class.

Features of Structure Classes (2)

- Unlike form classes which carry lexical meaning, structure classes carry functional or grammatical meaning.
- They signal the functional relationships among other words.
  - In "John received a gift from Mary," from has the function of identifying Mary as the source of the gift.

of -mean nothing

Incomplete Inventory of Structure Classes

- Determiners
- Pronouns
- Prepositions
- Auxiliaries
- Degree Adverbs
- Coordinating Conjunctions

_____

_____

_____

_____

_____

_____

_____

Determiners

Words that co-occur with nouns

Features of Determiners

- Determiners share a common distribution.
  - They occur in pre-nominal position.
    - the course their grades Tom's report
- Determiners are constituents of a NP.
- Determiners modify the head noun.
- Determiners are generally the first constituent of a NP.
  - the exceptionally boring book

Sub-categories of Determiners

- Articles
  - a, an, the
- Possessive Determiners
  - my your his her its our your (pl) our
- Possessive nouns
  - Mary's children's

(handwritten notes)

before noun within a noun phrase

dets
a, an, the

adj
very

parts inside of NP

Sub-categories of Determiners(2)

- Demonstratives
  - this that these those *shows distance*
- ~~Quantifying Determiners~~ *indefinites*
  - any every some each other
- WH- determiners
  - whose which

More on Quantifying Determiners

- Some quantifying determiners distinguish count nouns from non-count nouns.
- For example, the determiner <u>both</u> has the inherent meaning of more than one but less than three; therefore, it can only modify count nouns:
  - both books
  - *both water

More on Quantifying Determiners

- <u>Much</u> and <u>many are a</u> contrastive pair because the first only modifies non-count nouns and the latter modifies count nouns:
  - I do not have much time to study.
  - *I do not have much hours to study.
  - I do not have many hours to study.
  - *I do not have many time to study.

count nouns can have numbers infront of it

Determiners as NP Substitutes

- Some determiners can have a second function--That of NP substitute.
- NP substitutes can take the place of an entire NP; they function just like pronouns.

Types of NP Substitutes

- Possessive nouns
  - Richard's grades are good, but Jim's are better.
- Demonstratives
  - These articles are informative, but those are more current.
- Quantifying Determiners (not all of them)
  - Some students study hard, and some do not.

Jim's grades — *whole pro form*

substitutes for those articles

Type of pro form is any word that can substitute for whole phrase

---

More on NP Substitutes

- Determiners generally introduce a NP, but NP substitutes are single words that take the place of entire NPs.
  - Most doctors are competent, but some are not.
- Most is a determiner, but some is a NP sub.

Exercises
to follow

Exercises

- Determine if each underlined word below is a determiner or a NP substitute.
  - His first class starts at 8:00 in the morning.
  - Jim's lawyer wants to file the motion, but Drew's does not.
  - The designers hate these drawings but like those.

The Distribution of Determiners

- Determiners are mutually exclusive before the same head; only one can modify a noun.
  - *my the book   *the this book   *a some book
- This regularity appears to be violated by some NPs that contain possessive nouns.
  - the elephant's trunk

NPs with Possessive Nouns

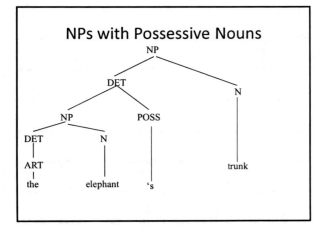

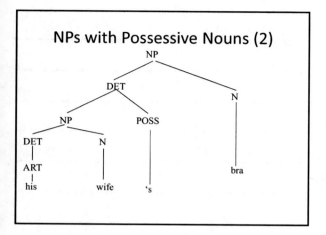

NPs with Possessive Nouns (2)

Pronouns

Single Words that
Substitute for
Noun Phrases

handwritten: pronouns substitute entire noun phrases

Types of Pronouns

- Subject Pronouns
- Object Pronouns
- Possessive Pronouns
- Reflexive Pronouns
- Others to be presented later
  - Interrogative Pronouns
  - Relative Pronouns

The Semantic Features of Pronouns

- Person refers to the situational characteristics of the participants in a conversation
  - First person--the one who is speaking *handwritten: I, we*
  - Second person--the one who is being addressed *handwritten: you, y'all*
  - Third person--person or entity being referred to *handwritten: he, she, it, they*
- Number
  - Singular
  - Plural
- Gender
  - Masculine
  - Feminine *handwritten: only in 3rd person*
  - Neuter *handwritten: he she it neuter*

130

Subject and Object Pronouns

	Subject Pronouns	Object Pronouns
1st Person Singular	I	me
2nd Person Singular	you	you
3rd Per. Singular M.	he	him
3rd Per. Singular F.	she	her
3rd Per. Singular N.	it	it
1st Person Plural	we	us
2nd Person Plural	you	you
3rd Person Plural	they	them

Possessive and Reflexive Pronouns

	Possessive Pronouns	Reflexive Pronouns
1st Person Singular	mine	myself
2nd Person Singular	yours	yourself
3rd Per. Singular M.	his	himself
3rd Per. Singular F.	hers	herself
3rd Per. Singular N.	---	itself
1st Person Plural	ours	ourselves
2nd Person Plural	yours	yourselves
3rd Person Plural	theirs	themselves

Distribution of Pronouns (1)

- Subject pronouns
  - Occur as the subjects of finite clauses *tensed verb shows inflection*
    - » Tom is a good student -->
    - » He is a good student
    - » Students know that Dr. Ray is a good instructor -->
    - » Students know that she is a good instructor

Distribution of Pronouns (2)

- Object pronouns
  - Occur as the objects of verbs and prepositions
    - The students liked the guest lecturers --> *noun phrase the object pron of verb*
    - The students liked them *verb*

    - The committee received a proposal from Dr. Ray --> *preposition*
    - The committee received a proposal from her

Distribution of Pronouns (3)

- Possessive pronouns
  - Occur in either subject or object position
    - Your courses seem interesting, but my courses are dull --> *noun phrase*
    - Your courses seem interesting, but mine are dull

    - Ambar likes her courses, but Fred doesn't like his courses -->
    - Ambar likes her courses, but Fred doesn't like his

Distribution of Pronouns (4)

- Reflexive pronouns
  - Occur as direct objects when they are co-referential to the subject
    - * The chemistry student burned themselves

    - The chemistry student burned himself

    - *We blamed themselves for the accident

    - We blamed ourselves for the accident

Grammatical Features of Pronouns (1)

- Agreement
  - Pronouns agree with their antecedents in person, number, and gender
    - When <u>Fred</u> took the exam, <u>he</u> looked worried
    - When <u>the students</u> took the exam, <u>they</u> looked worried
    - When <u>Mary</u> took the exam, <u>she</u> looked worried

---

Grammatical Features of Pronouns (2)

- Substitution
  - Pronouns substitute for entire noun phrases.
    - <u>The corpulent man with the artificial tan</u> is a professor of ethics
    - <u>He</u> is a professor of ethics
    - We received the manuscript from <u>the professor of linguistics</u>
    - We received the manuscript from <u>him</u>

Noun Phrase Boundaries

- Pronouns can be used to identify the boundaries of noun phrases.
  - She met the man in the green shirt
  - She met him
  - She met the man in the park
  - She met him in the park

Exercises

- Each sentence below has an underlined noun. Using pronoun substitution identify the boundaries of the noun phrase.

  - They bought the <u>bicycle</u> with the bent wheel

  - They bought the <u>bicycle</u> at the garage sale

  - The <u>people</u> in the auditorium began to cheer

  - The <u>man</u> who bought the coat returned it

  - We watched a <u>concert</u> in the park

Errors with Pronouns

- Even older writers make some agreement errors with pronouns.
- They get themselves into the following situation: They write a generalization using a singular subject and then refer to that singular subject with plural pronouns.
- The following are actual sentences written by university students.

Errors with Pronouns

- Once a child has realized the parameters of their language, they simply plug words in the proper order to form a sentence.
- Every person is born equipped with a Universal Grammar that tells them how to extract syntactic patterns out of the speech that they hear around them.

Errors with Pronouns

- Avoid the error by writing in the plural.
  - Once children have realized the parameters of their language, they simply plug words in the proper order to form a sentence.
  - All people are born equipped with a Universal Grammar that tells them how to extract syntactic patterns out of the speech that they hear around them.

Proforms

- A proform is a single word that substitutes for an entire phrase.
- Pronouns are just one type of proform in English.
  - Pronouns substitute for NPs
    - The man imitating a parakeet has eaten one too many bird seeds.
    - He has eaten one too many bird seeds.

Proforms

- As you will see in later sections, pronouns also substitute for any structure functioning nominally such as a noun clause.
- Any structure that has one of the six grammatical functions that a simple NP has is a nominal.
  - Whoever conducted this study made errors.
  - They made errors.

Other Proforms

- English also has proforms that substitute for structures functioning adverbially. The two most common are <u>then</u> and <u>there</u>.
  - <u>There</u> substitutes for adverbials of place.
    - Our friends were <u>at the concert</u> last night.
    - We were <u>there</u> too.
  - In the example above <u>at the concert</u> is a prepositional phrase functioning adverbially.

Other Proforms

  - <u>Then</u> substitutes for adverbials of time.
    - Our lecture started <u>at 6:00 p.m</u>.
    - Ours started <u>then</u> too.
  - In this example, <u>at 6:00 p.m</u>. is another prepositional phrase functioning adverbially.

Other Proforms

- English also has interrogative proforms.
- <u>Who</u> and <u>what</u> always elicit nominal responses.
  - Who discovered penicillin?
    - Dr. Fleming
  - What is penicillin?
    - The first antibiotic

Other Proforms

- <u>Where</u> and <u>when</u> elicit adverbial responses.
  - Where is Waterloo?
    - In Belgium
  - When was the Battle of Waterloo fought?
    - In 1815
- Other proforms will be discussed in subsequent sections.

Prepositions

Words that Begin Phrases

Features of Prepositions

- Prepositions are words that form phrases with a following noun phrase.
- Together they form a prepositional phrase:
  - <u>to</u> my friend
  - <u>in</u> the park
  - <u>behind</u> your back
  - <u>through</u> the window
  - <u>on</u> the job market

Features of Prepositions (2)

- The first word in a prepositional phrase is usually the preposition.
- The following noun phrase is the <u>object of the preposition</u>.
- If the object of the preposition is a pronoun, it always occurs in object form.
  - from Mary = from her
  - to my friends = to them

Phrasal Prepositions

- Some groups of words actually comprise a single preposition because they have the same function and distribution as one word prepositions. Below are a few examples:
  - instead of
  - because of
  - on account of
  - in addition to

Exercises

- Identify the prepositional phrases in the sentences below:
  - War and Peace is about most marriages.
  - "Rocky XXXVI" has great scenes of gnashing gums.
  - The store on the corner sells shrunken heads from the Amazon.
  - People hate to be put on hold.

Stranding Prepositions

- At some point in their educational career, most students have received a comment such as "don't strand prepositions" or "don't end a sentence with a preposition."
- Such statements are examples of prescriptive rules, rules of speaking and writing correctly under the assumption of an absolute standard of correctness.

Stranding Prepositions (2)

- This 'rule' of not stranding a preposition was artificially incorporated into the grammar of English by English grammarians in the 18th century.
- They took the rule from Latin. In Latin the stranding of a preposition does violate the grammar of the language and is thus ungrammatical.

Stranding Prepositions (3)

- Is the stranding of prepositional phrases grammatical in English?
- The answer is definitely yes.
- It is the necessary result of certain movement rules of English.
- WARNING: What follows is technical, and not for the grammatically infirm.

Stranding Prepositions (4)

- What are you talking about?
- The question above has a stranded preposition--about.
- About is stranded because English has a movement rule called Wh-movement which takes Wh words and moves them to the beginning of a clause.

Stranding Prepositions (5)

- The question actually started out as "You are talking about what?"
- If the Wh word is the object of a preposition, the preposition will be stranded.
- Notice that no other acceptable way really exists to utter or write the question.

_____

_____

_____

_____

_____

_____

Stranding Prepositions (6)

- You might be tempted to say : "About what are you talking?"
- Though such remedies might work at times, they usually sound unnatural and affected.
- So if an instructor says "don't strand prepositions," say "you don't know what you are talking about."

_____

_____

_____

_____

_____

_____

Stranding Prepositions (7)

- The previous statement is our course frivolous.
- The non-stranding of prepositions has become the standard in Edited American English, and some English teachers and editors will mark sentences containing stranded prepositions as wrong.

_____

_____

_____

_____

_____

_____

Stranding Prepositions (8)

- Finally then, the stranding of prepositions is not ungrammatical, and speakers of English strand them every day.
- However, in formal writing the stranding of prepositions is not the preferred choice stylistically even if it is grammatical.

Stranding Prepositions (9)

- When grading papers, remember the difference between style and grammar.
- Do not let students believe that they are writing ungrammatically when what you really want to say is that they should use a different style.

Auxiliaries

Words that Form Verb Groups

What are Auxiliaries?

- Auxiliaries occur with each other and main verbs to form verb groups.
  - A verb group is a main verb and all of its auxiliaries, if any.
    - should have been eaten
    - should have eaten
    - should eat
    - ate
- Auxiliaries and their combinations convey such information as tense, aspect, and voice.

maximum word group
 # ae 3
Main verb is always
the Last verb of the
Sentence.

Properties of all Auxiliaries

- The first auxiliary of a verb group and the subject of the clause can be inverted to form questions.
  - Maritza has lived in Spain.
  - Has Maritza lived in Spain?
  - Nigel can speak Zulu.
  - Can Nigel speak Zulu?

Spilt verb group

asking yes/no ? can
helep you find aux.

Properties of all Auxiliaries (2)

- The first auxiliary of the verb group attracts the negative.
  - Ambar has traveled extensively.
  - Ambar has not traveled extensively.
  - Your family is coming to dinner.
  - Your family is not coming to dinner.

the 1st verb group

Negative Particle is
Not
simple test of finding
auxilary

Properties of all Auxiliaries (3)

- Auxiliaries can act as predicate substitutes. *aux*
  - Nigel can speak Ainu, and Mirabel can too. *aux*
  - Fred has purchased a new car, and Alejandra has too.

predict

verb group

Properties of all Auxiliaries (4)

- Auxiliaries appear in short answers.
  - Can Nigel speak Swahili?
  - Yes, he can. → *aux.*
  - Have you seen "Rocky XXI"?
  - Yes, I have → *aux.*

Types of Auxiliaries

- Modal auxiliaries   10
- Primary auxiliaries   have, be   2
- Dummy auxiliary   do

all share the same 4 properties as long as their the 1st aux of the verb group.

Modal Auxiliaries

- will   ↔   • would
- can   ↔   • could
- shall   ↔   • should
- may   ↔   • might
- must
- ought to

4 pairs

Modal Auxiliaries (2)

- None of the modal auxiliaries are inflected   do not
  - he swims
  - *he cans swim
- The modals are followed by a verb in base infinitive form
  - can go
- Only one can appear in a verb group.
  - *Tom will can swim.
- If they occur in a verb group, they are first.

to recieve Full infinative base = Recieve
to swim
to go

will + can both aux.

Primary Auxiliaries

- The two primary auxiliaries are <u>have</u> and <u>be</u>.
- Both auxiliaries are conjugated, but they are irregular.
  - have has had
  - am are is was were

Primary Auxiliaries (2)

- Both primary auxiliaries can co-occur with the modals; when they do, they appear after the modals.
  - should have studied *primary aux*
  - might (be) studying
- The two can co-occur with each other; when this happens, <u>have</u> is first.
  - have been sleeping

Primary Auxiliaries (3)

- The verb that follows <u>have</u> must be in the perfect participle form.
  - have eaten
- The verb that follows <u>be</u> must be in the ~~passive~~ *Past* participle form or the ~~progressive~~ *Present* participle form.
  - is eating
  - was eaten

primary aux   MV

The Dummy Auxiliary

- Remember the four properties that all auxiliaries share in common.
  - The first auxiliary and the subject invert to form questions
  - The first auxiliary attracts the negative
  - Auxiliaries can substitute for predicates
  - Auxiliaries appear in short answers

Discovering the Dummy Auxiliary

- Convert the following sentences to negative statements and questions; by doing so, you will discover the dummy auxiliary.
  - Most athletes train daily.
  - Tom's aunt owns a houseboat.
  - The police caught the suspect.

You need an auxiliary verb to make negative or questions

DO

More Questions

- What is the dummy auxiliary? *do*
- Why is it used? *Make Verbal sys.*
- What does it mean? *Nothing.*
- Is the dummy auxiliary conjugated? *yes did, done, does*
- In what form is the verb that follows the dummy auxiliary? *did have infinite true form*
- Does the dummy auxiliary occur in only the simple present tense and the past tense?

yes

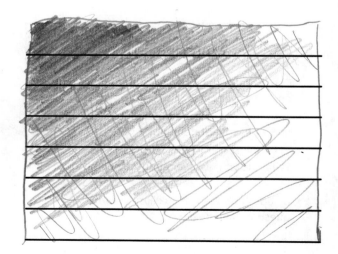

Lexical Verbs or Auxiliaries?

Main

- Read the following sentences and decide if the underlined words are lexical verbs or auxiliaries.
  - My brother <u>has</u> the flu. = Lexical
  - John <u>is</u> crazy. lexical
  - The kids <u>did</u> their homework quickly. = Lexical
- None are auxiliaries; if a verb group consists of one verb, it is always the main verb.

Verb group consit of 1 word

Lexical Verbs or Auxiliaries?

- Because <u>have</u>, <u>be</u> and <u>do</u> are both lexical verbs and and auxiliaries, they can appear

  in the same verb group together.
  - My brother <u>has</u> had the flu. the last word is the main verb trad
  - John <u>is</u> being crazy. being
  - The kids <u>did</u> not do their homework quickly.
    do

forms of have

More about <u>Be</u>

Main

- The lexical verb <u>be</u> behaves differently from any other verb in English.
- Turn the following statement into a question and a negative statement.
  - His wife <u>is</u> a doctor.
- What did you discover about the behavior of <u>be</u>?
- <u>Be</u> does not need an auxiliary to form questions and negative statements.

His wife is not a doc.
Is his wife a doc.

Be has the characteris of aux

Degree Adverbs (Qualifiers)

A Type of Pre-Modifier

A Partial Inventory of Degree Adverbs

- quite
- very
- so
- too
- rather
- really
- less
- least

- somewhat
- more
- most
- still
- pretty
- even
- kind of
- sort of

Functions of Degree Adverbs

- Degree adverbs modify gradable adjectives
  - quite hot
  - very thirsty
  - so fast
  - too expensive
- They do not modify non-gradable adjectives
  - *very dead
  - *too pregnant
  - *quite last
  - *so first

Functions of Degree Adverbs(2)

- Degree adverbs also modify general adverbs derived from gradable adjectives.
  - <u>very</u> quickly
  - <u>too</u> rapidly
  - <u>quite</u> emotionally
  - <u>somewhat</u> intelligently

Functions of Degree Adverbs (3)

- Degree adverbs do not modify general adverbs derived from non-gradable adjectives.
  - *very absolutely
  - *too uniquely
- Some linguistic approaches classify general adverbs derived from non-gradable adjectives as degree adverbs.

Distribution of Degree Adverbs

- Degree adverbs appear only before the word that they modify; they are pre-modifiers
  - They looked at him <u>very</u> oddly.
  - This room is <u>too</u> hot.
  - Fred is <u>sort of</u> lazy.

premodifers
never heads of their own
phrases

Distribution of Degree Adverbs (2)

- Degree adverbs never appear alone.
  - *They looked at him <u>very</u>.
  - *This room is <u>too</u>.
  - *Fred is <u>sort of</u>.
- Degree adverbs never modify each other.
  - *They looked at him <u>very too</u> oddly.
  - *This room is <u>too quite</u> cold.
  - *Fred is <u>sort of rather</u> lazy.

Testing for Degree Adverbs

- Because degree adverbs always appear in particular positions and have a particular function, you can test for them by the substitution of <u>very</u>.
  - The book is <u>quite</u> boring.
  - The book is <u>very</u> boring.
- Because <u>very</u> successfully substitutes for <u>quite</u>, <u>quite</u> is also a degree adverb.

very

A Problem with Substitution

- General adverbs can also modify adjectives.
  - <u>oddly</u> inconclusive
  - <u>obviously</u> awkward
  - <u>remarkably</u> clear
- Remember that degree adverbs can occur in the same position.
  - <u>quite</u> inconclusive
  - <u>very</u> awkward
  - <u>so</u> clear

A Problem with Substitution (2)

If both degree adverbs and general adverbs can modify adjectives, how can you tell the difference between the two?

* {I Y} general adverb

Possible Answers to the Problem of Substitution

- Think semantically:
  - General adverbs ascribe many types of characteristics to the adjectives they modify. they describe a characteristic by <u>kind</u>.
    - diabolically hot   *great romantic, saying alot*
- Degree adverbs demonstrate the <u>extent</u> to which the adjective is realized.
  - very hot   *not saying alot*

Preliminaries to the Best Solution for the Problem

- Remember the following points:
  - Both degree adverbs and general adverbs can modify adjectives.
  - Degree adverbs can modify general adverbs derived from gradable adjectives.
  - Degree adverbs do not modify one another or general adverbs derived from gradable adjectives.

very quickly

* too very

The Best Solution

- Examine the following sentence:
  - The answer was <u>oddly</u> inconclusive.
- <u>Inconclusive</u> is an adjective modified by <u>oddly</u> which could be either a degree adverb or a general adverb.

The Best Solution (2)

- Try modifying <u>oddly</u> with a degree adverb such as <u>very</u>.
- If the resulting phrase is grammatical, then <u>oddly</u> is a general adverb that has been derived from a gradable adjective:
  - very oddly

Exercises

- Determine if the underlined words below are degree adverbs or general adverbs:
  - Most graduate students are <u>extremely</u> intelligent. *degree*
  - The statue is <u>strikingly</u> beautiful. *general*
  - The answers are <u>obviously</u> incorrect. *general*
  - The questions were <u>too</u> difficult. *degree*
  - The students were <u>quite</u> surprised. *degree*

Coordinating Conjunctions

Words that Connect Constituents
Together

An Inventory of Coordinating Conjunctions

- and
- but
- or
- nor
- for
- yet
- so

The Function of Conjunctions

- Coordinating conjunctions conjoin constituents of equal grammatical structure together.
- For example, a noun phrase can be conjoined to another noun phrase .

Examples of the Function of Coordinating Conjunctions

- Noun Phrases
  - Tom <u>and</u> Jerry are cartoon characters.
  - Americans like tasty food <u>and</u> tasteless movies.
- Adjective Phrases
  - The novels of Tolstoy are exceptionally long, <u>but</u> exceptionally good.
  - It's possible to be sad, <u>but</u> rich.

Examples of the Function of Coordinating Conjunctions (2)

- Prepositional Phrases
  - We can eat in the Japanese restaurant, <u>or</u> in the Italian one.
  - Some people jog in the morning <u>and</u> in the evening.
- Clauses
  - They went to the Grand Canyon, <u>for</u> they had never seen it.
  - Dr. Johnson became ill, <u>so</u> he canceled class.

Errors with Coordinating Conjunctions

- Two phrases that are different in grammatical structure may not be conjoined.
  - Tom likes to run in the morning and lifting weights in the afternoon.
    - The above sentence is ungrammatical because it conjoins an infinitive phrase with a gerund phrase.

Errors with Coordinating Conjunctions

- The ungrammatical sentence can be repaired by making both phrases infinitives or gerunds.
  - Tom likes to run in the morning and to lift weights in the afternoon.
  - Tom likes running in the morning and lifting weights in the afternoon.

More on the Functions of Coordinating Conjunctions

- For sentences with coordinating conjunctions to be grammatical the conjoined phrases must be identical in grammatical structure as just discussed.
- Conjoined phrases must be identical in another way. In the following example a sentence conjoins two prepositional phrases, yet the result is ungrammatical.

Exercise

- The first two sentences below are grammatical but the third is not. Why not?
  - Merry wrote an article on Virginia Woolf.
  - Merry wrote an article on vacation
  - *Merry wrote an article on Virginia Woolf and on vacation.

Burn Gray
Matter

156

Grammatical Function

- The third sentence in the preceding exercise is ungrammatical because one prepositional phrase is functioning adjectivally and the other adverbially.
- Conjoined phrases must have equal grammatical structure and equal grammatical function.

Lectures
in
Syntax

Introduction to Syntax

How Phrases and Clauses
are Constructed

Purposes of this Section

- To define the concept of phrase.
- To identify different types of phrases.
- To describe the internal structure of phrases.
- To define the concept of constituent. — part
- To distinguish between optional and
  obligatory constituents.   *tense deleted*

  ↓
  cant be deleted

Purposes of this Section

- To identify the functions of the different
  phrases acting as constituents.
- To present techniques for identifying the
  constituents in a clause.

*techniques – movement, deletion,
substitution (syntactic analysis)*

Phrases

What are Phrases?

phrase

- A sequence of words that has a particular word as its head.
  - Note, however, that some of them may consist of a single word.
- The internal structure of the phrase follows specific patterns that conform to the grammar of the language.
- The phrase functions as a unit.

more, delete + substitute

a phrase consist of just a single word

if any
head noun and all modifiers
if any, some phrases consist
of just a single word

The Internal Structure of Phrases

- All phrases are endocentric.
  - Each phrase has a head. *specific word that makes the phrase what it is*
  - Phrases are maximal projections of the head. *(can modify)*
  - The head determines the type of phrase it is.
    - A noun is a head of a noun phrase.

162

Types of Phrases

- Noun Phrase (NP)
- Adjective Phrase (AP)
- Adverb Phrase (AvP)
- Prepositional Phrase (PP)
- Verb Phrase (VP)

noun or proform

The Noun Phrase

- The NP consists of a head noun and all of its modifiers, if any.
- According to this definition, a NP can consist of many words or a single word.
  - The hiker who fell off the cliff during the storm was badly injured. _single NP & modifier_
  - The hiker was badly injured.
  - He was badly injured.

proform   _one word noun phrase_

The Noun Phrase

- A one way dependency exists between a noun and its modifiers.
- A NP must have a noun, but it does not have to have any modifiers. _adj phrase_
  - Nancy bought a very rare book.
  - Nancy bought a book.
  - *Nancy bought a very rare.

can delete the adj phrase and it still would be grammatical But can't delete the noun phrase

The Adjective Phrase

- An AP consists of a head adjective and all of its modifiers, <u>if any</u>.
- Again, a AP may consist of a single word or many.
  - The students were <u>very happy with their grades</u>.
  - The students were <u>very happy</u>.
  - The students were <u>happy</u> .

The Adjective Phrase

- A one way dependency exists between an adjective and its modifiers.
- An AP must have an adjective, but it does not have to have any modifiers.
  - The oven was <u>very hot</u>.
  - The oven was <u>hot</u>.
  - *The oven was <u>very</u>.

Handwritten note: can eliminate modifiers, but can't delete heads & keep modifier. will be ungrammatical

The Adverb Phrase

- An AvP consists of a head adverb and all of its modifiers, if any.
- An AvP may consist of several words or just one.
  - The instructor spoke <u>too quickly by far</u>.
  - The instructor spoke <u>too quickly</u>.
  - The instructor spoke <u>quickly</u>.

The Adverb Phrase

- A one way dependency exists between an adverb and its modifiers.
- An AvP must have an adverb, but it does not have to have any modifiers.
  - Some people drive too slowly.
  - Some people drive slowly.
  - *Some people drive too.

can eliminate modifiers, but can't delete adverb and keep modifier; will be ungrammatical

Prepositional Phrases

- A prepositional phrase consists of a preposition and a complement called the object of the preposition.
- The object of the preposition is a noun phrase or a noun phrase substitute.
  - from the terrace —np
  - on the stairs — np acting as the object of the preposition

prep

Prepositional Phrases

1st   2nd

- Every preposition has an object which generally follows the preposition.
- Sometimes movement rules extract the object, but it is always recoverable.
  - Luis is from Chile.
  - Where is Luis from?
    - Where is the object of the preposition even though it does not follow the preposition.

— the object of the prep. will follow prep

wh movement, move them to beginning clause

Prepositional Phrases

- The preposition and its object are in a state of <u>mutual dependency.</u>
- For a PP to exist, it must have both a preposition and an object.
  - We received a letter from Spain.
  - *We received a letter from.
  - *We received a letter Spain.

[handwritten: not like others]

The Verb Phrase

- A VP consists of a verb group and all of its complements and modifiers, if any.
- The verb group and its modifiers are in a condition of one way dependency.
  - The runner <u>stumbled awkwardly.</u>
  - The runner <u>stumbled.</u>
  - *The runner <u>awkwardly.</u>

[handwritten: VG, VP]
[handwritten: 7 no compliments]
[handwritten: doesn't have a verb phrase]

[handwritten: complements – follow the main verb that can't be deleted]

The Verb Phrase

- A verb group consists of a head verb and all of its auxiliaries, if any.
- The main verb and auxiliaries are in a condition of one way dependency.
  - should have been studying
  - should be studying
  - should study
  - study

[handwritten: every VP must have a VG in it]

Constituents

What are Constituents?

- Any structure that participates in making up a larger structure is a constituent of that larger structure. *(part)*
  - NPs, APs, AvPs, VPs and PPs are the constituents *(parts)* of sentences.
  - Words are the constituents of phrases.
- Every phrase in a clause is a phrasal constituent. *(part of the clause)*

parts that make sentences

Phrases as Constituents

- Clauses are constructed of phrases intermediate between the highest node--the S--and the ultimate constituents--the words.

```
           S
         /   \
       Ph     Ph
      /  \    /  \
     w    w  w    w
```

All words have to be part of phrases and all phrases have to be part of sentences

The Order of Constituents

- Constituents are arranged in specifiable and predictable orders.
  - S ---> NP VP _sentence NP determine adj noun PNP._
  - NP ---> (Det) (AP) N (PP)
  - PP ---> P NP

All has to go in order

Optional Constituents

- Optional constituents are those that can be deleted from a sentence.
- Deletable constituents are not needed for a sentence to be grammatical.
  - We had dinner after the concert last night.
  - We had dinner after the concert.
  - We had dinner.

Obligatory Constituents

- Obligatory constituents are those that cannot be deleted from a clause. _(sentence)_
- They are needed for the clause to be grammatically complete.
  - The tornado destroyed the bridge.
  - *destroyed the bridge
  - *the tornado the bridge   _ungrammatical_
  - *the tornado destroyed

Functions of Phrasal Constituents

- Each type of phrasal constituent has a specifiable range of functions.
- The VP is always the predicate.
- APs, AvPs, and PPs are modifiers.

each type of phrase has a predictable order

Functions of Phrasal Constituents

- The NP has six different functions:
  - Subject of Verb (SV)
  - Direct Object (DO)
  - Indirect Object (IO)
  - Subject Complement (SC)
  - Object Complement (OC)
  - Object of Preposition (OP)

The Functions of NPs

- The function of a NP depends upon its relationship to other elements in a S.
  - The king was coronated *SV*
  - Someone tried to assassinate the king. *DO*
  - The queen gave the king a gift. *Indirect do*
  - That man is the king. *SC*
  - The people made Leopold the king. *OC*
  - A letter arrived from the king. *OP*

Subject and Predicate

- The two immediate constituents of a clause are the NP functioning as the SV and the VP functioning as predicate.
  - S ---> NP VP
- The NP and the VP are in a relationship of mutual dependency. The function of one can only be determined through the presence of the other.

eaten by analigators —
isn't a clause needs a NP

Identifying Subject and Predicate in Statements

- Find the verb group; everything to the left is the subject. The predicate is the VG and everything to its right. NP   VGT
  - The instructor of the last class has forgotten his notes.
    - Verb group = has forgotten
    - SV = The instructor of the last class
    - VP = has forgotten his notes

Find the verb group
left - subject
VGT and to the right is the predicate

Identifying Subject and Predicate

declarative
- Find the subject and predicate in the simple sentences below: NP   VGT   VP
  - The subjects of sentences are easy to find.
  - WWII lasted from 1939 to 1945.
  - The first human occupants of the Americas arrived here 13,000 years ago. VGT
  - The atomic number of an atom is its total number of protons. VGT

NP - can't always trade w/
pronoun/ proform

Problems with Declarative Sentences: Sentence Adverbials

- Some declarative sentences may begin with a sentence adverbial.
  - Suddenly, the fire alarm sounded. *pred .*
  - In 1492, Columbus landed in Cuba. *pred .*
- Sentence adverbials are not part of the subject; simply move them to the end of the sentence as in the following slide.

Problems with Declarative Sentences: Sentence Adverbials = *predicate*

  - Suddenly, the fire alarm sounded. →
  - The fire alarm sounded suddenly.
    - Verb Group = sounded
    - SV = the fire alarm
    - VP = sounded suddenly

Problems with Declarative Sentences: Predicate Adverbials

- Some declarative sentences have a predicate adverb between the subject and the verb group.
  - Napoleon never should have invaded Russia. *VG → predicate adverb*
- The SV is the NP before the verb group.
- Because never is not part of the NP, it is not part of the subject.

Problems with Declarative Sentences: Predicate Adverbials

- You can see that <u>never</u> is not part of the NP by using pronoun substitution.
  - Napoleon never should have invaded Russia. →
  - He never should have invaded Russia.
- The pronoun substitutes for <u>Napoleon</u>, not for <u>Napoleon never</u>.

Sentences with Adverbials

- Find the subject and predicate in the sentences below.
  - After the revolution Russia became an industrialized nation.
  - Unfortunately, many people lost their homes in the hurricane.
  - In the United States 50,000 people are shot with hand guns every year.

Identifying Subject and Predicate in Yes/No Questions

- Whatever is between the first auxiliary and the rest of the verb group is the SV.
  - Are politicians financing their campaigns legally?
    - Verb group = are financing
    - SV = politicians
    - VP = are financing their campaigns legally

Identifying Subject and Predicate in Yes/No Questions

- Find the subject and predicate in the following yes/no questions.
  - Has the United States found weapons of mass destruction in Iraq?
  - Did the horse become extinct in the Americas?
  - Can chimpanzees manufacture tools?

A Problem with Yes/No Questions

- Yes/no questions with the copula do not have an auxiliary.
  - Is your family at home?
- How would you find the SV?
  - Turn the question into a statement.
  - Find the verb group.
  - Everything to the left is the SV.

- Turn the question into a statement to find the NP

Yes/No Questions with the Copula

- Find the subject and predicate in the sentences below.
  - Are sub-atomic particles visible?
  - Were the questions easy on the test?
  - Are student textbooks too expensive?
  - Is phi really the golden ratio?

Wh questions

The Subject and Predicate in Content Questions

- With one exception content questions are like yes/no questions—the subject is found between the first auxiliary and the rest of the verb group.
  - When will hydrogen be a dependable source of energy?
  - Why is the universe expanding?

most wh split verb group

A Problem with Content Questions

- When content questions question the subject position, no auxiliary is used.
  - Who wrote the article?   *turn the question into a statement*
- To find the subject, create a statement using a NP for the WH word.
  - Chomsky wrote the article.
- Chomsky is the SV in the statement, so who is the SV in the question.

If don't find split verb group in wh questions the wh is the subject itself by replacing wh w/ name

A Problem with Content Questions

- If the copula is the main verb in a content question, the subject of the sentence may occur after the verb group.
  - What is the capital of Canada?
- In this question, the subject is 'the capital of Canada.'

A Problem with Content Questions

- The subject seems to appear in an unusual position because of two movement rules. First, the subject inverts with the verb; then WH movement applies.
  - the capital of Canada is what →
  - is the capital of Canada what →
  - What is the capital of Canada?

Practice with Content Questions

- Find the subjects and predicates in the following content questions.
  - Why did you miss class?
  - Who discovered penicillin?
  - Which class did you miss?
  - When did the dodo become extinct?
  - What is the longest river in the world?

Grammatical and Logical Subjects

- So far we have identified the subject as the NP, or NP substitute, that occupies a specific syntactic position in sentences. This is the **grammatical subject**, and all sentences in English have a grammatical subject.

Grammatical and Logical Subjects

- English has two words that can be the grammatical subjects of sentences: <u>it</u> and <u>there</u>.
  - There are too many people in New York.
  - It is apparent that the students studied hard.
- <u>It</u> and <u>there</u> are the grammatical subjects, but they are also devoid of semantic content.

can't define there *& it ex. semantic content*

Grammatical and Logical Subjects

- Because <u>there</u> and <u>it</u> are devoid of semantic content, they are dummy subjects, not the <u>logical subjects.</u>
- The logical subjects have been moved to a different location in the sentence.
  - A girl is in my soup --->
  - is a girl in my soup --->
  - There is a girl in my soup.

dummy   logical
Gramm
subject

Grammatical and Logical Subjects

- In nearly all clauses the logical subject and the grammatical subject are identical.
- Only when clauses have dummy subjects are the grammatical subject and the logical subject different from each other.

Grammatical and Logical Subjects

- Find the grammatical and logical subjects in the sentences below.
  - The atomic number of uranium is 92.
  - There is a hare in my spaghetti.
  - It is obvious that the administration has launched an attack on legitimate science in the United States.

Manipulating Constituents

Tests for identifying the boundaries of constituents

The Manipulation of Constituents

- Only phrases can be manipulated.
  - Deletion
  - Movement
  - Substitution
- If a sequence of words is deleted, moved, or replaced by a single word and the result is a grammatical structure, the sequence is a phrase.

AP &
where a NP begins & end

The Manipulation of Constituents

- If sentences were not composed of phrasal constituents, then any se-quence of words would be manipulable.
  - They walked to campus in the morning.
  - In the morning they walked to campus.
  - *Morning they walked to campus in the.
  - *Campus in the they walked to morning.

phrasal const.

can only move phrasal constituents

Substitution

- Many constituents can be replaced by a single word called a proform.
- Pronouns are a type of proform.
  - The magician who performed the most amazing tricks to raise money for poor Republicans who couldn't get accepted into country clubs made himself disappear.
  - He made himself disappear.

single noun phrase, this type of substitution

using pronoun subs, can show us where an NP begins & ends

Substitution

- Pronoun substitution can determine if a PP is inside or outside of a NP.
  - She met the man in the sunglasses. *PP*
  - She met him.
  - She met the man in the park.
  - She met him in the park. *adverbial*
- In the sunglasses is part of the NP, but in the park is not.

Practicing with Substitution

- Using pronoun substitution, find the NPs in the following sentences.
  - The queen abdicated. *she*
  - Those two people taught the history course. *it* *they*
  - Many young kids wear oversized jeans. *them* *they*
  - A few students left their books.
    they *them*

Practicing with Substitution

- Using pronoun substitution, decide whether the following prepositional phrases are modifiers in a NP *them*
  - We left the papers on the desk. *prep. adverb*
  - I write my papers on a computer. *them* *prep adv*
  - The text for the course is expensive. *post modifier noun* → *prep. phrase functions adjective;*
  - I met the faculty of linguistics. *pos mod. noun*

Deletion

- Deletion is useful for finding the optional constituents of a sentence.
- What can be eliminated from the following sentence?
  - Because it was going to rain, the students walked very quickly to the library. *optional constituents.*
- Optional constituents include PPs, APs, AvPs and some clauses.

* amount of optional constituents is relevant

Practice with Deletion

- Using deletion, decide if the underlined structures are optional constituents.
  - Some politicians are honest. *no*
  - We watched the news last night. *yes*
  - The alarm went off too early. *yes*
  - For the most part, modifiers are optional *yes* constituents.
  - NPs are not optional constituents. *no*

Movement

- If a sequence of words can be moved as a unit, the sequence is a constituent.
- Movement is especially useful for identifying adverbial modifiers.
  - Last election, less than 40% of the registered voting population actually voted.
  - Less than 40% of the registered voting population actually voted last election.

adverbial modifier

Practice with Movement

- Using movement, find the adverbial modifiers below.
  - Many people exercise to lose weight.
  - If you have some time later, you can help me.
  - In 1944, the Allies landed in Normandy.
  - The East India Company lost control of India after the Sepoy Rebellion.

Main Verbs and Their Complements

Identifying types of sentences
in English

Verb Groups: A Review

- All sentences in English must have a verb group.
- The verb group must minimally consist of a main verb; auxiliaries are optional.
- Main verbs can be sub-categorized depending on the number of complements they require and the types of complements.

Verb Groups: A Review

- Complements of main verbs are constituents that appear after the main verbs and are required to complete the predicate.
- The main verb is so important in English sentences that the names for the different types of sentences are taken from the main verbs that are in them.

Types of Sentences 5

- Intransitive 0 complement contain
- Intensive 1 comp. a type of
- Monotransitive 1 comp. verbs
- Ditransitive 2 comp.
- Complex transitive 2 complements

subj
direct
direct/indirect
direct/object

Intransitive Sentences

- Intransitive sentences have intransitive verbs as their main verbs.
- Intransitive verbs do not require a complement to complete the predicate.
- Any constituent following an intransitive verb is an optional modifier.
- These modifiers can be deleted, so the sentence can end with the main verb.

Intransitive Sentences

- Examples of intransitive sentences:
  - They have been sitting for a long time.
  - They have been sitting.
  - Most politicians lie like rugs.
  - Most politicians lie.
  - Dr. Smith faints at the sight of blood.
  - Dr. Smith faints.

* look for main verb
if what follows is optional
if it's optional than it's
intransitive

A Warning

- Never delete a NP; it has a grammatical function.
  - Fred ate turkey. ← *direct object*
  - Fred ate.
- If you delete turkey, your answer will be that the sentence is intransitive.

consider all NP as obligatory!

never delete a pronoun or noun clause

Some Advice

- To find sentence types, always begin by locating the main verb first.
- To do the practice sentences that follow, begin by identifying the main verb.

Practice

- Discover which of the sentences below are intransitives. Try deletion.
  - The tornado destroyed the trailer park. *NP not intransitive*
  - Queen Victoria died in 1901. *intransitive*
  - His dog choked on a cat bone. *intransitive*
  - They put their wet coats on the couch. *NP not*
  - He smoked for two decades. *intransitive*
  - She was reading in the library. *intransitive*

don't take a complement, ends in the intransitive verb

Intensive Sentences

- The complement of an intensive verb is called a subject complement because it supplies additional information about the subject of the sentence.
- Intensive verbs are also referred to as linking verbs.
- The most frequently occurring intensive verb is the copula, be.

use be to test or some sort of be

Intensive Sentences

◆ Type of Verb
  – Intensive

◆ Type of phrase
  – NP
  – AP
  – NPadv
  – PP

Intensive Sentences

- You do not need to memorize all of the intensive verbs in English.
- If you can substitute some form of the verb be for the main verb in a sentence and get approximately the same meaning, then you found another intensive verb.

be substitution
=

Finding Other Intensive Verbs

- Using <u>be</u> substitution, find the other intensive verbs below.
  - The students [seem] tired today. _are_ _intensive_
  - The ex-felon [became] a politician. _are_ _intensive_
  - We [met] the professor of the class. _is_ _not_
  - The dinner [looks] good. _is_ _intensive_
  - George W. Bush [hated] the illogical speaker. _not_

NP as Subject Complement

- When a NP is a subject complement, it is coreferential with the SV.
- When NPs are coreferential, they each refer to the same entity.
  - Tolstoy is a Russian author.
  - Tolstoy = a Russian author.
  - $NP_1 = NP_2$
- Only NPs can be coreferential. _— only NP_

_NP = NP_

NP as Subject Complement

- The NP that is subject complement must agree in number with the subject of the sentence. _singular_ _singular_
  - John became a phonologist.
  - *John and Mary became a phonologist.
  - John and Mary became phonologists.
  - *John became phonologists.

AP as Subject Complement

- When an AP is subject complement, it modifies the SV.
  - The movie sounds awful.
  - The examination seems easy.
- You can test for the adjective by moving it to a position of premodification.
  - the awful movie
  - the easy examination

PP as Subject Complement

- When a PP is the subject complement, it modifies the SV.
  - The concert was in the park.
  - The elderly patient appears in good health.

NPadv as Subject Complement

- The subject complement can also be a NP functioning adverbially. These are NPs of time and place.
- The main verb in these cases is almost always be.
  - The game was yesterday.
  - The test will be tomorrow.
  - The noise was downstairs.

NPadv as Subject Complement

- These NPs are functioning adverbially because an adverbial proform can substitute for them.
  - My examination was yesterday
    - Mine was then too.
  - My examination is tomorrow.
    - Mine is then too.
  - The noise was downstairs.
    - The noise was there.

then - time

there - place

Some Advice

- If some form of be is the main verb of a sentence, then the sentence will always be intensive.
- If some form of be can substitute for a main verb, then the sentence is intensive.

SC - the word after the verb

Practice

- Find the intensive verbs below and identify the type of phrase that constitutes the SC.
  - The class seems lost today. intensive SC - lost can delete today
  - His daughter became a doctor. intensive SC - A doctor
  - Hannibal was a military genius. intensive SC - a military genius
  - A rose by any other name is still a rose. intensive - a rose
  - Warring nations can later become allies. intensive SC - allies
    be

187

A Note on Intensive Sentences and Modifiers

◆ Phrases that are modifiers include PPs, APs, NPadv and AdvPs.

• Most modifying phrases are optional constituents and can be deleted.

• However, modifying phrases that are subject complements are not optional constituents and cannot be deleted.

A Note on Intensive Sentences and Modifiers

• The underlined phrases below are all modifiers, but they are not optional because they are SCs.

   – The book you want is <u>in the new book room</u>. (PP) SC

   – Because of the storm, many of their possessions were <u>lost</u>. (AP) SC

   – The exam was yesterday. (NPadv) SC

Practice

• Determine if the sentences below are intensive.

   – Neanderthals were cousins of homo sapiens. *intensive*

   – The last Neanderthals died about 25,000 years ago. *not can delete the PP*

   – Some people are allergic to shell fish. *Intensive*

   – Few genetic mutations produce harmful effects. *not are*

Monotransitive Sentences

- Monotransitive sentences contain a monotransitive verb.
- A monotransitive verb is one that requires a single NP to complement it.
- This NP is the direct object of the verb.
  - One percent of Americans earn doctoral degrees.
    - verb = earn
    - DO = doctoral degrees

 *direct object*

The Direct Object

- Traditionally, the direct object is said to receive the action of the verb.
  - The DO is the recipient of the action.
- Examine the following sentence:
  - The mailman kicked our watch-iguana.
- The DO in this sentence is <u>our watch-iguana</u>, and it receives the action expressed in the verb <u>kick</u>.

The Relationship between SV and DO

- In intensive sentences the NP that is the SC is always coreferential to the NP functioning as SV.
  - My uncle is a dentist.
- In monotransitive sentences the NP that is the DO is not coreferential with the NP functioning as SV.
  - My uncle married a dentist.

An Exception

- The DO can be coreferential with the SV only if the DO is expressed as a reflexive pronoun.
  - The dog bit itself.
  - The speaker corrected himself.
  - Dictators elect themselves.

Testing for Monotransitive Sentences

- If a verb is followed by a single NP, the NP is either a SC or a DO
- Test by <u>be</u> substitution; if it works, the NP is a SC; if it does not work, it is a DO.
  - His family [bought] a new car. *monotransitive a new car = DO*
    - Be substitution --->
  - His family is a new car.

Practice

- Using <u>be</u> substitution, decide if the sentences below are intensive or monotransitive.
  - Their children all [became] professionals. *intensive*
  - Sharks will [eat] almost anything. *monotransitive*
  - They [grow] tomatoes in the backyard. *mono*
  - The couple [remained] friends after the divorce. *intensive*

Testing for Monotransitive Sentences

- Monotransitive sentences are active sentences; the SV is the agent of the action.
- Most monotransitive sentences can be transformed into passive sentences.
  - The judge fined the drunk driver.
  - The drunk driver was fined by the judge.

How to Form Passive Sentences

- Make the DO of the active sentence the SV of the passive sentence.
- Express the SV of the active sentence as the object of <u>by</u> in the passive sentence.
- Form a passive verb group--some form of the verb <u>be</u> followed by the main verb in passive participle form.

Example of the Passive Transformation

◆ The dog bit the bellicose cat.

◆ The bellicose cat was bitten by the dog.

Practice

- Transform the active monotransitive sentences below into passives.
  - The hurricane destroyed the fishing fleet.
  - John Wilkes Booth assassinated President Lincoln in 1865.
  - Many people admire good Samaritans.
  - The instructor's assistant read the lectures.

The Semantic Relationship between Actives and Passives

- Active and passive sentences have dramatically different structures, yet they are synonymous. why?
- The answer involves the notion of thematic roles carried by NPs.
- In addition to having a grammatical function, a NP has a thematic role--a semantic interpretation.

The Semantic Relationship between Actives and Passives

- In active sentences, the SV is the <u>agent</u> of the action, and the DO is the <u>recipient</u> of the action.
  - The cat ate the bird.
- In forming passive sentences, grammatical functions change, but not the thematic roles assigned to the NPs.
  - The bird was eaten by the cat.

The Semantic Relationship between Actives and Passives

- Meaning changes if the thematic roles assigned to the NPs change.
  - The dog bit the cat.
  - The dog was bitten by the cat.
- In both sentences, the dog is the SV, yet the sentences are not synonymous.
- The dog is the agent in the first, and the recipient in the second.

Practice

- Find the NPs in the pairs of sentences below and identify the thematic roles and the grammatical functions of each.
  - The parrot killed the cat. *Active*
  - The cat was killed by the parrot. *passive*
  - Florida sued the tobacco industry. *Active*
  - The tobacco industry was sued by Florida. *passive*

Ditransitive Sentences

- Ditransitive verbs take two NPs as complements.
  - Verb NP NP
- The first complement is the IO.
- The second complement is the DO.
  - John gave Mary a poisoned cactus.
    - Mary is the IO
    - a poisoned cactus is the DO

Ditransitive Sentences

- The IO can follow the DO, but only if it is preceded by the object marker to or for.
  - John read Mary the book
  - John read the book to Mary.
  - John bought Mary a book.
  - John bought a book for Mary.

A Note on to and for.

- The object markers to and for mark the IO; the prepositions to and for create modifying phrases.
- Find the markers and prepositions below.
  - John sent a letter to Spain. preposition
  - John sent a letter to Mary.
  - John bought a book for Mary.
  - John bought a book for six dollars. → preposition

More on the DO and IO

- The DO and the IO are not coreferential.
  - John read Mary the book.
    - Mary is not the book.
  - The used car salesman sold Mortimer a lemon.
    - Mortimer is not a lemon.

Practice

- Find the DO and the IO in each of the sentences below:
  - Texaco now gives promotions to minorities
  - The judge gave the drunk driver a very heavy fine.
  - The father threw the baseball to his son.
  - Fred sold his uncle a car.

Ditransitive Sentences and the Thematic Roles of NPs

- The SV is the agent.
  - The agent performs the action.
- The DO is the recipient.
  - The recipient directly undergoes the action of the verb.
- The IO is the beneficiary.
  - The beneficiary benefits from the action.

Making Passives from Ditransitives

- Ditransitive sentences can also be transformed into passives.
- In such cases, the SV is not the agent.
  - Monarchs gave land to the nobility.
  - The nobility was given land by monarchs.
  - Land was given to the nobility by monarchs.

Practice: Active to Passive

- Transform the ditransitive sentences below into passives, and identify the thematic roles of the NPs.
  - Cortez's troops gave diseases to the Aztecs.
  - Some parents throw lavish birthday parties for their children.
  - Some volunteers make soup for the poor.

General Practice

- Identify the sentence type of each sentence below.
  - Old soldiers never die. *intransitive*
  - The Acropolis is in Athens. *intensive — the Athens — SC*
  - Mars was the god of war. *intensive — god of war — SC*
  - Napoleon gave very small pensions to his enlisted men. *DO — ditransitive — DO only exists in ditransitive sent*
  - Male lions eat the young of other males. *monotransitive*

Complex Transitive Sentences

- Complex transitive verbs take two complements to complete the predicate.
- The first is a NP which functions as the DO of the verb.
- ◆ The second is a NP, AP, NPadv, or PP which functions as the Object Complement (OC).
- If the OC is a NP, it is coreferential with the DO.

Complex Transitive Sentences

SV	DO	OC
NP	NP	NP
		AP
		NPadv
		PP

Complex Transitive Sentences

- Examples of complex transitives:
  - The students called Nixon Tricky Dickey. (NP)
  - The architects considered the project impossible. (AP)
  - The husband put the trash outside. (NPadv)
  - Children always put their toys in the wrong places. (PP)

Testing for Complex Transitive Sentences

- Because both ditransitive verbs and complex transitive verbs can be followed by two NPs, it is possible to confuse the two structures.
- The DO and IO after ditransitive verbs are not coreferential.
  - Fred gave Mary a present.
  - Mary =/= a present

Testing for Complex Transitive Sentences

- The DO and the OC after complex transitive verbs are coreferential.
  - The students called Nixon Tricky Dickey.
    - Nixon = Tricky Dickey
  - The fourth grade elected Harry president.
    - Harry = president

Testing for Complex Transitive Sentences

- An intensive relationship exists between the DO and the OC.
  - The architects considered the project impossible.
    - the project is impossible
  - The husband put the trash outside.
    - the trash is outside
  - Children put their toys in the wrong places.
    - their toys are in the wrong place

Practice

- Decide if the following sentences are ditransitive or complex transitive.
  - The department members elected Dr. Smythe chairperson. *Dr smythe = chairperson complex*
  - The administration gave Dr. Badnews an award. *ditransitive*
  - The faculty consider Dr. Badnews a fraud. *complex*
  - Dr. Badnews read the faculty his unimpressive paper. *ditransitive*

Making Passives
from Complex Transitives

- Because complex transitive sentences have DOs, they can be passivized.
  - The students called Nixon Tricky Dickey. *Active*
    - Nixon was called Tricky Dickey. *Passive*
  - The architects considered the project impossible.
    - The project was considered impossible
  - The husband put the trash outside.
    - The trash was put outside.

Practice

- Transform the following complex transitive sentences into passives.
  - The committee appointed Dr. Smythe chairperson.
  - The faculty consider Dean Johnson a good administrator.
  - The fourth graders elected Fred classroom representative.
  - Nancy called John an ugly name.

Review of Sentence Types

- There are five basic sentence types.
  - Intransitive
  - Intensive
  - Monotransitive
  - Ditransitive
  - Complex transitive

Review of Sentence Types

- Sentence types are named after the main verb that each contains.
- Verbs differ on the number and types of complements that they can take.
- Intransitive verbs do not take a complement, so the sentence can end in the main verb.

Review of Sentence Types

- ◆ Intensive sentences need a SC to complete the predicate. The SC may be a NP, AP, NPadv, or PP.
  - Discover intensive verbs by <u>be</u> substitution.
- Monotransitive sentences need a DO to complete the predicate. The DO is a NP.
  - <u>Be</u> substitution does not work.

Review of Sentence Types

- Ditransitive sentences take a IO and DO as complements. Both complements are NPs.
  - The IO can come second if marked by <u>to</u> or <u>for</u>.
- Complex transitive sentences take a DO and OC as complements. The DO is a NP.

Review of Sentence Types

- The OC is a NP, AP, AvP, or PP.
  - There is an intensive relationship between the DO and the OC.
- Only transitive sentences can be made passive.

Practice

- Identify the sentence type of the following sentences. Work together.
  - Many people become disillusioned with their jobs.
  - Mr. Johnson resigned abruptly yesterday.
  - The Vikings established a settlement on North America long before Columbus.
  - Very few immigrants receive welfare.

Phrasal Verbs

Single verbs consisting of more
than one word

Discovering Phrasal Verbs

- Identify the main verb in each sentence below.
  - The neighbors put out the fire.
  - The nervous child turned on the light.
  - The tired dancer took off her shoes.
  - Steve has already brought in the newspaper.

Discovering Phrasal Verbs

- The neighbors <u>put out</u> the fire.
- The nervous child <u>turned on</u> the light.
- The tired dancer <u>took off</u> her shoes.
- Steve has already <u>brought in</u> the newspaper.
- What type of sentences are these?

Discovering Phrasal Verbs

- Each of the sentences is transitive because each one can be transformed into a passive.
- Only transitive sentences can be transformed into passives.
  - The fire was put out.
  - The light was turned on.
  - The shoes were taken off.
  - The newspaper was already brought in.

Discovering More

- Look at the sentences again. Can you change the word order in another way without making them passive?
  - The neighbors put out the fire.
  - The nervous child turned on the light.
  - The tired dancer took off her shoes.
  - Steve has already brought in the newspaper.

Particle Movement

- The example sentences can be restated as follows:
  - The neighbors put the fire out.
  - The nervous child turned the light on.
  - The tired dancer took her shoes off.
  - Steve has already brought the newspaper in.
- The second word of this type of phrasal verbs is called a particle.
- Particles can move around a direct object.

Transitive with Particle

- We shall call this type of phrasal verb a transitive with particle.
- This type of phrasal verb is transitive because sentences containing them can be made passive.
- They are unique in that the last element in them--the particle--can move around the direct object of the sentence.

Discovering Other Phrasal Verbs

- Identify the main verb in each sentence below.
  - The doctor called on the elderly patient.
  - The authorities attended to the complaint.
  - The adversaries consented to the proposal.
  - The committee hinted at a possible compromise.

Discovering Other Phrasal Verbs

  - The doctor called on the elderly patient.
  - The authorities attended to the complaint.
  - The adversaries consented to the proposal.
  - The committee hinted at a possible compromise.
- What type of sentences are these?
- Each of these sentences is transitive.
- Each one contains a phrasal verb that is followed by a direct object.

Discovering Other Phrasal Verbs

- The sentences are transitive because each one can be transformed into a passive.
    - The elderly patient was called on by the doctor.
    - The complaint was attended to by the authorities.
    - The proposal was consented to by the adversaries.
    - A possible compromise was hinted at by the committee.

Discovering Other Phrasal Verbs

- Look at the sentences again. Is the second element of the phrasal verb a particle?
    - The doctor called on the elderly patient.
    - The authorities attended to the complaint.
    - The adversaries consented to the proposal.
    - The committee hinted at a possible compromise.

Discovering Other Phrasal Verbs

- *The doctor called the elderly patient on.
- *The authorities attended the complaint to.
- *The adversaries consented the proposal to.
- *The committee hinted a possible compromise at.
- Movement of the second word results in ungrammatical sentences, so the moved element is not a particle.

Phrasal Transitives

- We will call the second type of phrasal verb a phrasal transitive.
- Like the transitive with particle, this type of phrasal verb is transitive because it takes a direct object and can be made passive.
- Unlike the transitive with particle, the second element of the phrasal verb cannot move around the direct object.

One More Type of Phrasal Verb

- Identify the main verb in each sentence below.
  - The fighter gave up after the third round.
  - The storm let up suddenly after six hours.
  - The plane took off on time.

One More Type of Phrasal Verb

  - The fighter gave up after the third round.
  - The storm let up suddenly after six hours.
  - The plane took off on time.
- What type of sentences are these?
- Each sentence is intransitive because each can end with the main verb.
  - The fighter gave up.
  - The storm let up.
  - The plane took off .

Phrasal Intransitives

- This last type of verb will be called a phrasal intransitive.
- As is true of all intransitive verbs, none of them require a complement to complete the predicate.

Exercises

- Find the phrasal verb in each sentence and identify what type of verb it is.
  - Hearing a noise, we looked up quickly.
  - The man yelled at the children.
  - Some students were standing up in the class.
  - The investors put up the money.
  - Fluorescent condoms light up your life.

The Functions of Noun Phrases

The Six Functions

- NPs in English have six general functions.

– SV	SC	DO
– IO	OC	OP

object *inside VP* *when noun phrase follows somethin*

- The functions of NPs can be determined by their position in phrases and clauses:

SV

Subj. verb

- The SV in statements is always before the verb group.
  - Athens is in Greece.

- The SV in most questions is between the first auxiliary and the rest of the verb group.
  - Have the workers gone on strike?

aux *verb*

SC

- NPs that are SCs always occur after intensive verbs.

  main verb be; become substitute for

  - Most professors are good scholars.
  - Many people with doctoral degrees become professors.

DO

- NPs that are DOs always occur after transitive verbs: mono-transitive, ditransitive, and complex transitive.

  - Dr. James wrote a manuscript. *mono be subt. fails*
  - He sent the manuscript to a publisher. *ditransitive*
  - The publisher put it in the trash. *complex*

IO

- A NP that is a IO always occur with ditransitive verbs.

  can move IO before or after DO w/ to or for

  - Dr. Smith gave his students a very long examination.
  - Dr. Smith gave a very long examination to his students.

IO

- Note that the IO always occurs with a DO and may precede or follow it.

  - Josh sent <u>his brother</u> a letter.
  - Josh sent a letter to <u>his brother</u>.

OC

- NPs that are OCs <u>always occur with a complex transitive verb.</u>

  - The mayor named his best friend <u>chief of police</u>.

    [handwritten: DO above "his best friend"; NP below "his best friend"; NP below "chief of police"]

- Note that the OC always follows the DO.

OP

- NPs that are OPs normally <u>occur after a</u> preposition.

  - The Roman Empire fell in <u>the fifth century</u>.
  - The last emperor of <u>Rome</u> was Romulus Augustulus.

Testing for NPs

- You can discover NPs with pronoun substitution.
  - Many political bureaucracies are poorly organized.
    - They are poorly organized.
  - The first people to colonize the Americas crossed the Bering Strait.
    - They crossed it.

Testing for NPs

- NPs always answer questions with <u>who</u> and <u>what</u>.
  - English is a West Germanic language.
    - What is English?
    - a West Germanic language *N P*
  - Alexander the Great invaded Persia.
    - Who invaded Persia?
    - Alexander the Great *NP*

Exercises

- Find the NPs in each sentence and identify their functions. *subj DO*
  - The Moors invaded Spain in the eighth century. *OP*
  - The Moors were actually Berbers. *SUD comple*
  - *subj* They became Muslims and fought with the Arabs. *OP*
  - In Spain, the Moors founded many towns. *DO*
  - The Spanish drove out the Moors in 1492.
  - *subject   DO   OP*

The Functions of Prepositional Phrases

Distinguishing between optional and obligatory constituents

Prepositional Phrases as Modifiers

- Prepositional phrases are always modifiers.
  - They restrict the interpretation of the constituent that they modify.
    - the house
    - the house with shingles
    - the house with shingles on the corner
    - the house with shingles on the corner of Oak street

restrict the interpretions of what they modify

Prepositional Phrases as Obligatory Modifiers

- Some prepositional phrases are obligatory.
  - If they are deleted from a sentence, the remaining structure will be ungrammatical.
    - The conference is in the auditorium.
    - * The conference is
    - They put the books on the top shelf.
    - * They put the books
- Prepositional phrases are obligatory when they are subject or object complements.

Prepositional Phrases as Optional Modifiers

- When prepositional phrases are optional modifiers, they can be deleted from a sentence, and the remaining sentence will be grammatical.
- The track team was training in the park.
  - The track team was training.
- Note that the second sentence has less information because it contains one less modifier, but it is still grammatical.

The Functions of Prepositional Phrases as Optional Modifiers

- Postmodifier of a noun (adjectival modifier)
  - A prepositional phrase can follow a noun and modify that noun.
    - the book with the red cover
    - a flight into space
    - friends in high places
    - a short book about honest politicians
    - a long book about scandalous politicians

modifies a noun

Testing for Postmodifiers of Nouns

- Because a postmodifier of a noun must follow the noun that it modifies, it may never be moved to the beginning of the sentence.
  - We all need friends in high places.
    - *In high places we all need friends.
  - The text on paleoanthropology is required.
    - On paleoanthropology the text is required.

can't move prep phrase to beginning of sentence w/ postmodifier

Testing for Postmodifiers of Nouns

- Because a postmodifier of a noun is part of a NP, pronoun substitution can be used to discover whether a PP is part of a NP or not.
  - He met <u>the professor of linguistics</u>.
  - He met her.
  - * He met her of linguistics.
  - She saw <u>the professor</u> in the library.
  - She saw him in the library.

Practice

- Determine whether the underlined PPs are postmodifiers of nouns.
  - John took a course <u>on Victorian history</u>. Postmodifiers
  - The instructor taught the course <u>in the evening</u>. adverbrall y
  - The students bought some textbooks <u>at a discount</u>. adverbrall y
  - The other textbooks <u>for the course</u> were very expensive. post modifiers

The Functions of Prepositional Phrases as Optional Modifiers

- Postmodifier of an adjective
  - A PP can follow an adjective and modify the adjective.
    - The students were happy <u>with their grades</u>.
    - The President was pleased <u>with the compromise</u>.
    - Many people are angry <u>at Congress</u>.
    - Many other people are content <u>with Congress</u>.

Testing for Postmodifiers of Adjectives

- Because a PP functioning as a postmodifier of an adjective must follow an adjective, it cannot be moved to the beginning of the sentence.
  - The students were happy with their grades.
    - **With their grades the students were happy.
  - Many Americans are unhappy about the war.
    - **About the war many people are unhappy.

The Functions of Prepositional Phrases as Optional Modifiers

- Adverbial modifier
  - If a PP is not a postmodifier of a noun or adjective, then it is functioning adverbially.
    - The students went home after the exam.
    - Dresden was destroyed in 1945.
    - I met my friend in the library.
    - The press was skeptical after the interview.
  - Note that PPs functioning adverbially can even follow a noun.

Testing for Adverbials

- If a PP can be moved to the beginning of a sentence, or already occurs at the beginning, it is functioning adverbially.
    - William the Bastard defeated the English in 1066.
    - In 1066, William the Bastard defeated the English.
    - Dresden was destroyed in 1945.
    - In 1945, Dresden was destroyed.
    - In the summer, many Americans travel.

Testing for Adverbials

- Not all PPs functioning adverbially can be moved to the beginning of the sentence.
- If a PP occurs after any type of word other than a noun or adjective, it is an adverbial.
- If a PP occurs after a noun, but is not in the NP, it is functioning adverbially.
  - They finished the work <u>by noon.</u>
  - They finished it <u>by noon.</u>

Testing for Adverbials

- PPs phrases funcioning as adverbials frequently answer questions with <u>when</u> and <u>where</u>.
  - After the Battle of Hastings, William started to consolidate his rule of England.
  - When did William begin to consolidate his rule of England?
  - After the Battle of Hastings.

Testing for Adverbials

  - Venice is on the northwestern coast of Italy.
  - Where is Venice?
  - On the northwestern coast of Italy.

Summary of the Functions of Prepositional Phrases

- Obligatory modifiers
  - subject complement
  - object complement
- Optional modifiers
  - postmodifier of a noun
  - postmodifier of an adj.
  - adverbial

Exercises

- Find the function of each underlined PP
  - They ate lunch <u>in the park</u>. *adv*
  - The book <u>about Greek history</u> is <u>on the table</u>. *Postadj* *adv* *SC*
  - <u>From the mountains</u>, you can see <u>for a long way</u>. *adv*
  - They put the manuscripts <u>in the rare book room</u>. *OC*
  - The students were unhappy <u>about the exam</u>. *postadj*

End of Exercises

- End of prepositional phrases

217

Finite Subordinate Clauses

Clauses within Larger Sentences

Features of Subordinate Clauses

- Like all clauses, FSCs have a subject and a predicate.
- Unlike independent clauses, FSCs cannot stand on their own.
  - when the class is over
- FSCs begin with a word that makes the clauses incapable of being independent.
- FSCs have a tensed verb group.

Types of Finite Subordinate Clauses

- Adverb clauses
- Adjective clauses
- Noun clauses
- That clauses

Adverb Clauses

Examples of Adverb Clauses

- <u>When most college students graduate</u>, they get a job.
- The Union won the Civil War <u>because it had a superiority in manufacturing and population.</u>
- <u>Even though South Africa called itself a democracy</u>, only a minority could vote.

beginning at sentence setoff w/a comma
& come at the end of sentence

The Internal Structure of Adverb Clauses

- Adverb clauses begin with a subordinating conjunction, such as
  - <u>when</u> <u>because</u> and <u>even though</u>
    - Name some other subordinating conjunctions
- If you delete the subordinating conjunction, the remaining structure reads as if it were an independent clause.

where as if after

The Internal Structure
of Adverb Clauses

- when most college students graduate, →
  - most college students graduate
- because the Union had a superiority in manufacturing and population →
  - the Union had a superiority in manufacturing and population
- even though South Africa called itself a democracy
  - South Africa called itself a democracy

The Function of Adverb Clauses

- Adverb clauses modify the independent clauses with which they are associated.
- They do so because of the subordinating conjunction.

The Function of Adverb Clauses

- The subordinating conjunction establishes the semantic relationship between the content of the adverb clause and the main clause.
- For example, the subordinating conjunction *if* expresses a conditional relationship:
  - If I were your wife, I would put poison is your coffee.
  - And if I were your husband, I would drink it.
    - (exchange between Mary Astor and Winston Churchill)

Choosing the Correct Subordinating Conjunction in Writing

- Because subordinating conjunctions are strong in semantic content, writers must choose the one best expressing the intended meaning.
- Young writers frequently use such subordinating conjunctions as <u>since</u> and <u>as</u> for cause and effect.

Choosing the Correct Subordinating Conjunction in Writing

- The sentences are strengthened by using <u>because</u>:
  - As the stock market is currently in decline, many investors are getting out.
  - Since the stock market is currently in decline, many investors are getting out.
  - Because the stock market is currently in decline, many investors are getting out.

The Function of Adverb Clauses

- Because adverb clauses are adverbials, they can answer such adverbial questions as <u>when</u> and <u>why</u>.
  - After the stock market crashed in 1929, the United States entered a depression.
    - When did the United States enter a depression?
    - After the stock market crashed in 1929.
  - Because early prehistoric settlers over hunted, the horse became extinct in the Americas.
    - Why did the horse come extinct in the Americas?
    - Because early prehistoric settlers over hunted.

Testing for Adverb Clauses

- Because adverb clauses are optional modifiers, they can be deleted from a sentence.
  - If you arrive early, we can study together.
  - We can study together.
- Because these clauses function adverbially, they can be moved around the main clause.
  - We can study together if you arrive early.

Exercise

- Find the adverb clause in each sentence.
  - Before you can receive a license, you have to pass two examinations.
  - Even though few people know it, many Chilean wines are both good and inexpensive.
  - Hurricanes are worse than tornadoes because hurricanes can have tornadoes inside of them.
  - While you were outside, someone called.

Adjective Clauses

Postmodifiers of a noun

Examples of Adjective Clauses

- The writer who sent the manuscript is a professor of Victorian history.
- I read the book that you didn't like.
- The students who received the lowest grades complained.

has their own subject & predicate w/in the clause

The Function of Relative Clauses

- Relative clauses function adjectivally; they modify the head noun of a NP.
- They are postmodifiers of a noun.
  - The man who was shot just robbed a bank
- Though the clause must follow the noun, it need not always follow immediately.
  - The man in the green hat who was shot just robbed a bank

Adjective Clauses and Pronoun Substitution

- Because adjective clauses are postmodifiers of nouns, a pronoun may be substituted for the entire NP.
  - The people who designed the test were fired.
  - They were fired.
  - We met the instructors who were teaching the course.
  - We met them.

Testing for Adjective Clauses

- Because adjective clauses are optional modifiers, they can be deleted.
  - He ruined the soup that he tried to make.
  - He ruined the soup.
- Because adjective clauses are postmodifiers, they can never be moved to initial position.
  - *That he tried to make he ruined the soup.

The Internal Structure of Adjective Clauses

- Adjective clauses begin with a relativizer.
  - Relative pronouns
    - who whom which that
  - Relative determiner
    - whose
  - Relative adverbs
    - where when

The Grammatical Function of Relative Pronouns

- Relativizers have a grammatical function in their own clause.
- As do all pronouns, relative pronouns substitute for a NP, and they have the same grammatical function as the NP for which they substitute.
- The NP for which the relative pronoun substitutes is a copy of the antecedent.

The Antecedent

- The noun, and all of its other modifiers, that the adjective clause modifies is called the antecedent.
  - The man who was shot just robbed a bank.
  - The man in the green hat who was shot just robbed a bank.
- The concept of antecedent is very important for understanding the internal structure of the adjective clause.

_____

_____

_____

_____

_____

Finding the Function of the Relative Pronoun

- To find the grammatical function of a relative pronoun, reconstruct the adjective clause by putting a copy of the antecedent into the clause and removing the relative pronoun.
- The reconstructed adjective clause will now look like an independent clause.

_____

_____

_____

_____

_____

Finding the Function of the Relative Pronoun

- I enjoyed the article [that you wrote] --->
- [you wrote the article]
- The article is the DO of the adj. clause.
- Therefore, that--the relative pronoun for the article--is also the DO in its own clause.
- Note that it is the copy of the antecedent which becomes relativized and then moved to the front of the adjective clause.

_____

_____

_____

_____

_____

_____

Practice

- Find the grammatical function of each relative pronoun. Work together. Don't look at the answers.
  - The course that he teaches is full.
  - I met the person who wrote the article.
  - The movie that Tom saw was awful.
  - The doctor whom we met was a surgeon.

End of Practice

- We's been relativized

More on Relative Pronouns

- A relative pronoun can be deleted if it is an object in its own clause.
  - The book that Tom wrote is awful.
  - The book Tom wrote is awful.
- This "missing" pronoun is called a zero relative pronoun, and it still has a grammatical function. In the sentence above it is a direct object.

The Other Relative Words

- <u>Whose</u> is always a relative possessive determiner in its own clause.
  - The writer <u>whose book we rejected</u> wrote a defamatory letter.
- The reconstructed relative clause is
  - we rejected the writer's book --->
  - we rejected whose book --->
  - whose book we rejected

_____

_____

_____

_____

_____

_____

_____

The Other Relative Words

- The relatives <u>when</u> and <u>where</u> are relative prepositional phrases in their own clauses.
  - The house <u>where Lincoln was born</u> was made into a museum.
- The reconstructed relative clause is
  - Lincoln was born in the house --->
  - Lincoln was born where --->
  - where Lincoln was born

_____

_____

_____

_____

_____

_____

_____

The Other Relative Words

- That <u>where</u> is a relative prepositional phrase can be proven by using a relative pronoun instead of <u>where</u>.
  - The house <u>that Lincoln was born in</u> is a museum
- When a relative pronoun is used, the preposition <u>in</u> surfaces in the sentence.
- The relative pronoun is the object of the preposition.

_____

_____

_____

_____

_____

_____

_____

Practice

- Decide whether the following sentences have an adjective or adverb clause.
  - We go to the store <u>when we need food.</u> _adverb_
  - I remember the year <u>when you were born.</u> _adj_
  - The children were frightened <u>after they saw the movie.</u> _adverb_
  - The students had to read an article <u>that their instructor wrote.</u> _adj_

Noun Clauses

Clauses that can have the same
functions as simple NPs

The Functions of Noun Clauses

- Noun clauses are NP substitutes.
- They appear in the same positions as simple noun phrases.
- They can have the same grammatical functions.
  - SV   DO   IO
  - SC   OP   OC

Examples of Noun Clauses

- <u>What I do</u> is my business. SV
- They don't know <u>what they should do</u>. DO
- The Red Cross gave assistance to <u>whoever needed it</u>. IO
- You can be <u>whatever you want</u>. SC
- The books are for <u>whoever wants them</u>. OP
- They called him <u>whatever they wanted</u>. OC

Internal Structure of Noun Clauses

- Noun clauses begin with a complementizer.
  - <u>what</u>   <u>whoever</u>   <u>whomever</u>
  - <u>whatever</u>   <u>whichever</u>
- Complementizers have a grammatical function in their own clause.
- Usually, but not always they have a nominal function.

Internal Structure of Noun Clauses

- <u>What I do</u> is my business.
  - <u>what</u> is a DO in its own clause.
- They don't know <u>what they should do</u>.
  - <u>What</u> is a DO in its own clause.
- The Red Cross gave assistance to <u>whoever needed it</u>.
  - <u>Whoever</u> is a SV in its own clause.

Internal Structure of Noun Clauses

- You can be <u>whatever you want</u>.
  - <u>Whatever</u> is a DO in its own clause.
- The books are for <u>whoever wants them</u>.
  - <u>Whoever</u> is a SV in its own clause.
- They called him <u>whatever they wanted</u>.
  - <u>Whatever</u> is a DO in its own clause.

Tests of Recognition

- Because noun clauses have a nominal function in the matrix sentence, they cannot be moved.
- Because noun clauses have a nominal function in the matrix sentence, they cannot be deleted.
- Because noun clauses have a nominal function in the matrix sentence, pronouns can substitute for them.

Practice

- Find the function of each noun clause in the sentences below; don't look at the answers.
  - I'll eat <u>whatever you want</u>. DO
  - The students didn't understand <u>what he said</u>. DO
  - SV — <u>Whatever solution is proposed</u> will be rejected.
  - We can give these clothes to <u>whoever wants</u> <u>them</u>. IO
  - She gives her children <u>whatever they want</u>. DO

Summarizing Tests of Recognition

- Deletion
  - Adjective clauses
  - Adverb clauses

- Movement
  - Adverb clauses
- Pronoun substitution
  - Noun clauses

_____

_____

_____

_____

_____

_____

_____

That Clauses

The Other Finite Subordinate Clause

Internal Structure of *That* Clauses

- *That* clauses begin with the complementizer <u>that</u>.
- The complementizer does not have a grammatical function in its own clause.
- <u>That</u> does not have any semantic content of its own.
- It merely signals that a subordinate clause is following.
  - I know <u>that</u> the answer is correct.

Internal Structure of *That* Clauses

- If <u>that</u> is covered, the rest of the clause appears to have the structure of an independent clause.
  - The students know <u>that the final is difficult</u>.
    - the final is difficult
  - Most Americans now realize that the tobacco industry has not issued honest reports.
    - the tobacco industry has not issued honest reports

Internal Structure of *That* Clauses

- <u>That</u> can be deleted from the that clause provided the clause is not the subject of the matrix sentence.
  - Most adults know that smoking is harmful to their health.
  - Most adults know smoking is harmful to their health.
  - That the rain will stop is doubtful.
  - *The rain will stop is doubtful.

The Functions of *That* Clauses

- Other finite subordinate clauses each have one particular function:
  - adjective clauses are postmodifiers of a noun
  - adverb clauses are adverbial modifiers
  - noun clauses are noun phrase substitutes
- *That* clauses have three general functions:
  - postmodifiers of nouns
  - postmodifiers of adjectives
  - some of the same functions as noun phrases

That Clauses as NP Substitutes

- *That* clauses can occupy some of the same positions as NPs and have some of the same functions.
  - SV
    - <u>That the students studied hard</u> is obvious.
  - DO
    - The students knew <u>that the exam would cover specific material</u>.
  - SC
    - The truth is <u>that the worst politician won</u>.

That Clauses as NP Substitutes

- As is true for all NPs, pronouns can substitute for that clauses.
  - That the students studied hard is obvious.
  - It is obvious.
  - The students knew that the exam would cover specific material.
  - The students knew it.
  - The truth is that the worst politician won.
  - The truth is this.

That Clauses as Postmodifiers of a Noun

- *That* clauses can follow and modify abstract nouns.
  - Many people have fears that they will lose their jobs.
  - The rumor that the company would close spread.
  - The fact that he failed the test caused him to drop the course.

That Clauses as Postmodifiers of a Noun

- Because postmodifiers of a noun are optional modifiers, they can be deleted from the sentence.
  - Many people have fears that they will lose their jobs.
    - Many people have fears.
  - The rumor that the company would close spread.
    - The rumor spread.

That Clauses as Postmodifiers of an Adjective

- *That* clauses can follow and modify adjectives.
  - The company is hopeful <u>that the shipment will arrive on time</u>.
  - The pollsters are sure <u>that the bond will be passed</u>.
  - The employees are fearful <u>that the manufacturer will lose the contract</u>.

That Clauses as Postmodifiers of an Adjective

- Because postmodifiers of an adjective are optional modifiers, they can be deleted from the sentence.
  - The company is hopeful <u>that the shipment will arrive on time</u>.
    - The company is hopeful.
  - The pollsters are sure <u>that the bond will be passed</u>.
    - The pollsters are sure.

Practice

- Find the *that* clause in each sentence below and identify its function. Work together.
  1 They didn't believe that the report was accurate.
  2 The students were happy that the course was over.
  3 That many politicians are dishonest is obvious.
  4 Her fears that she would do poorly were unfounded

Infinitive Clauses

A type of non-finite
subordinate clause

The Internal Structure
of Infinite Clauses

- The main verb of the infinitive clause is the infinitive.
  - to run   to speak   to understand
- The infinitive does not carry tense.
  - To vote is a right and a duty.
    - The infinitive does not take any inflectional endings that indicate tense, and it does not form verb groups with modal auxiliaries.

The Internal Structure
of Infinite Clauses

- For can be a complementizer introducing the infinitive clause.
- For must be present when the infinitive clause is the SV of the matrix sentence.
  - For the employees to accept pay cuts is unlikely.
  - *The employees to accept pay cuts is unlikely.

The Internal Structure of Infinite Clauses

- <u>For</u> may be optionally deleted when the infinitive clause is not the SV of the matrix sentence.
  - I would like for you to study more.
  - I would like you to study more.

The Internal Structure of Infinite Clauses

- The infinitive clause does not always have an overt subject.
- It is deleted when it is coreferential with the SV of the matrix sentence.
  - I would like you to study more.
  - I would like to study more.
  - He wants her to stop by the pharmacy.
  - He wants to stop by the pharmacy.

The Functions of Infinite Clauses

- Infinitive clauses have four basic functions:
  - NP substitute
  - Postmodifier of a noun
  - Postmodifier of an adjective
  - Adverbial modifier
- You can test for the functions with movement, deletion, and substitution.

Infinitive Clauses
as NP Substitutes

- Infinitive clauses can have many of the functions of simple NPs.
  - To run early in the morning is invigorating.
    - SV
  - They like to take trips to museums.
    - DO
  - The function of most bureaucrats is to engrandize their own meager positions.
    - SC

Infinitive Clauses
as NP Substitutes

- Just as NPs can be replaced by proforms, so can infinitive clauses.
  - To run early in the morning is invigorating.
    - It is invigorating.
  - They like to take trips to museums.
    - They like that.
  - The function of most bureaucrats is to engrandize their own meager position.
    - The function of most bureaucrats is this.

Practice

- Find the infinitive clauses below and determine if each is a SV, DO, or SC.
  - To be impartial is a necessity for a juror.
  - We need to go shopping.
  - The purpose of review exercises is to prepare students for the examinations.
  - Some students like to take their final examinations early.

Infinitive Clauses as Postmodifiers of a Noun

- Infinitive clauses can be postmodifiers of a noun.
    - No appeal <u>for the Red Cross to help</u> is ignored.
    - Your proposal <u>to have a take-home examination</u> is good.
    - "Ghandi" is a good movie <u>to see</u>.

Infinitive Clauses as Postmodifiers of a Noun

- Postmodifiers of an noun follow a noun.
- These infinitive clauses are optional modifiers and can be deleted.
    - No appeal <u>for the Red Cross to help</u> is ignored.
        - No appeal is ignored.
    - "Ghandi" is a good movie <u>to see</u>.
        - "Ghandi" is a good movie.

Practice

- Find the infinitive phrases functioning as postmodifiers of a noun. Use deletion.
    - Here is a book for you to read.
    - To read good literature is a virtue.
    - He has a good story to tell.
    - They want to visit many places.
    - Relativity is a difficult concept to understand.

Infinitive Clauses as Postmodifiers of an Adjective

- Infinitive clauses can be postmodifiers of an adjective.
  - The students were eager for the class to be over.
  - The instructor was happy to prepare the final examination.

Infinitive Clauses as Postmodifiers of an Adjective

- Postmodifiers of an adjective always follow an adjective.
- Because they are optional constituents, they can be deleted from the sentence.
  - The instructor was happy to prepare the final examination.
  - The instructor was happy.

Infinitive Clauses as Adverbial Modifiers

- Infinitive clauses can also be adverbial modifiers.
  - Many people swim to get exercise.
  - To receive a Ph.D., many graduate students study at least seven years.
  - To reduce the amount of street violence, the police imposed a curfew.

Infinitive Clauses as Adverbial Modifiers

- Adverbial modifiers are optional constituents and can be deleted.
  - Many people swim <u>to get exercise</u>.
    - Many people swim.
  - <u>To receive a Ph.D.</u>, many graduate students study at least seven years.
    - Many graduate students study at least seven years.

Infinitive Clauses as Adverbial Modifiers

- Many adverbial modifiers, unlike postmodifiers of nouns and adjectives, can be moved to initial position.
  - Many people swim <u>to get exercise</u>.
  - <u>To get exercise</u>, many people swim.
  - <u>To receive a Ph.D.</u>, many graduate students study at least seven years.
  - Many graduate students study at least seven years <u>to receive a Ph.D.</u>.

Infinitive Clauses as Adverbial Modifiers

- You can also find infinitive clauses functioning adverbially by placing <u>in order</u> in front of <u>to</u>.
  - Many people swim to get exercise.
  - Many people swim in order to get exercise.
  - Many people like to read.
  - *Many people like in order to read.

Practice

- Identify the infinitive clauses with the function of adverbials. Use deletion, movement, and <u>in order</u>.
  - They went to the store to buy some milk.
  - They need to finish the papers today.
  - Many students buy computers to write papers.
  - To increase production, the company increased hours.

Applying Manipulations

Summarizing Manipulations

- Substitution
  - NPs and NP substitutes
- Deletion
  - Optional modifiers
    - Adverbials
    - Postmodifiers of a noun or adjective
- Movement
  - Many types of adverbials

Testing with Manipulations

- Through the use of manipulations, you can test for the functions of structures that you may not even have studied.

_____

_____

_____

_____

_____

Practice

- Determine the functions of the under-lined structures. Work together.
  - The city <u>destroyed by the typhoon</u> was rebuilt.
  - <u>Exercising 20 minutes a day</u> is important.
  - Fred was chased by a dog <u>while running in the park</u>.
  - The mailman <u>bitten by the dog</u> sued the owner.

_____

_____

_____

_____

_____

_____

Identifying Grammatical Functions

Applying Manipulations

What You Do Not Know

- English has many syntactic structures that cannot be covered in an introductory course.
- The sentence below, for example, has a headless infinitive clause.
  - Tom needs to buy his textbook.
- Even though you do not know its name, you know that it is a NP substitute.

What You Do Know

- From the study of syntax you know that constituents of sentences can be manipulated in different ways depending upon their grammatical function.
- The three major manipulations are movement, deletion, and substitution.

entire phrases

What You Do Know (2)

- Optional constituents can be deleted from a sentence and the sentence will still be grammatical.
  - The students cheered <u>when the course ended</u>.
  - The students cheered.
  - <u>When the course ended</u> is an optional constituent.

What You Do Know (3)

- Optional constituents are usually modifiers:
  - Adverbials.
  - Postmodifiers of nouns.
  - Postmodifiers of adjectives.

What You Do Know (4)

- Obligatory constituents cannot be deleted from a sentence; the sentence will become ungrammatical.
  - <u>To vote in elections</u> is a duty.
  - *is a duty.
  - <u>To vote in elections</u> is an obligatory constituent because it cannot be deleted.

What You Do Know (5)

- Obligatory constituents are usually NPs and NP substitutes.
- They are any structure that have one of the typical NP functions:
  - SV   SC
  - DO   IO
  - OC   OP

Using Manipulations

- Manipulations can be used to distinguish adverbials, postmodifiers of nouns, postmodifiers of adjectives, and NP substitutes from one another.
- Different configurations of manipulations can be used to distinguish the four groups just mentioned.

Testing for Adverbials

- Because constituents functioning adverbially are generally optional modifiers, they can be deleted.
  - To understand syntax, students have to manipulate constituents.
  - Students have to manipulate constituents.

Testing for Adverbials (2)

- In addition, constituents functioning adverbially can normally be moved.
  - To understand syntax, students have to manipulate constituents.
  - Students have to manipulate constituents to understand syntax.

Testing for Postmodifiers of Nouns

- Because constituents functioning as postmodifiers of nouns are optional modifiers, they can be deleted.
  - St. Croix is a good place to take a vacation.
  - St. Croix is a good place.

Testing for Postmodifiers of Nouns (2)

- Postmodifiers of nouns cannot be moved to the front.
  - St. Croix is a good place to take a vacation.
  - * To take a vacation St. Croix is a good place.

Testing for Postmodifiers of Adjectives

- Because postmodifiers of adjectives contain optional information, they can be deleted from the sentence.
  - Intellectually active people are eager to learn new concepts.
  - Intellectually active people are eager.

Testing for Postmodifiers of Adjectives 2

- Because postmodifiers of adjective must follow the word that they modify, they cannot be moved to the beginning of the sentence.
  - Intellectually active people are eager to learn new concepts.
  - To learn new concepts intellectually active people are eager.

Testing for NP Substitutes

- Because NP substitutes have the same functions as NPs, pronouns can substitute for them.
  - Preparing a conference is a lot of work.
  - It is a lot of work.
  - The Italian government considered repairing the Leaning Tower of Pisa.
  - The Italian government considered it.

Testing for NP Substitutes (2)

- Because NP substitutes are obligatory constituents, they cannot be deleted from a sentence.
  - <u>Preparing a conference</u> is a lot of work.
  - *is a lot of work.
  - The Italian government considered <u>repairing the Leaning Tower of Pisa.</u>
  - *The Italian government considered.

Summarizing Tests of Recognition

- Deletion
  - Postmodifier of a noun
  - Postmodifier of an adjective
  - Adverbial
- Movement
  - Adverbial
- Pronoun substitution
  - Noun phrase substitute

If a structure can be moved & it's grammatical it adv.

anything that substitutes for NP

optional constituents will be grammatical

Exercises

- Each sentence on the following slide has an underlined constituent. Decide if the underlined constituent is a postmodifier of a noun, a postmodifier of an adjective, an adverbial, or a noun phrase substitute.

Exercises

- Many students enjoy <u>studying in the library</u>. N P
- <u>While examining the manuscript</u>, the editor *adverbize*
  found many errors.
- A good course <u>for prospective teachers to take</u>
  is sociolinguistics. *noun*
- The doctors treated the man <u>bitten by the black</u>
  <u>mamba</u>. *noun*
- Most people are happy <u>to go on vacation</u>.
  adj

Glossary

Glossary

adjectival A functional category. Adjectivals modify nouns; some such as adjectives appear in prenominal position (a *difficult* concept); others are postmodifiers of nouns such as prepositional phrases (the book *about linguistics*), adjective clauses (the book *that you received yesterday*), and *that* clauses (the idea *that the earth is round*); adjectivals may also appears after intensive verbs (The articles was *quite long*). Adjectivals are usually optional modifiers and can be deleted from a sentence without rendering the remainder ungrammatical.

adjective One of the four form classes. Adjectives modify nouns and are either gradable or non-gradable. **Gradable adjectives** such as *tall* and *small* take the comparative and superlative morpheme (*tall, taller, tallest*) and can be modified by degree adverbs (*very tall*). **Non-gradable adjectives** such as *dead* and *pregnant* do not take the comparative and superlative morphemes (*dead, *deader, *deadest*), and they cannot be modified by a degree adverb (**very dead*). Any word that can appear between a determiner and a noun is an adjective--*a _____ movie.*

adjective clause A finite subordinate clauses that functions as a post modifier of a noun. Adjective clauses normally begin with a relativizer, either a pronoun (*who, whom, that*), a determiner (*whose*) or a proform for a PP (*when* and *where*).

adjective phrase (AP) A head adjective and all of its modifiers, if any, as indicated in the following phase structure rule (premodifier) A (PP). In this case, the premodifier may be a degree adverb or a general adverb. Adjective phrases are usually optional modifiers and can consequently be deleted. They may not be deleted when they are subject and object complements.

adverb One of the four form classes. Although many adverbs are derived from adjectives by the derivational morpheme {-LY}, most adverbs cannot be identified by their morphology. Instead, adverbs are usually recognized by how they can be manipulated. Because they are optional modifiers, they can be deleted, but unlike other optional modifiers, such as adjectives, they can be moved as well. *Predicate adverbs* can move in the predicate, and *sentence adverbs* can by moved to sentence-initial or sentence-final position.

adverb clause A finite subordinate clause that functions adverbially. Adverb clauses may appear before or after the independent clause. They begin with a subordinating conjunction such as *if, whereas, because,* and *since.*

adverb phrase (ADVP) An adverb and all of its modifiers if any. The modifier of an adverb is a degree adverb: AdvP → (DA) Adv.

adverbial A functional category. Any structure that performs any of the same grammatical functions as an AdvP is an adverbial. Some PPs function adverbially as do all adverb clauses; some non-finite structures such as infinitive clauses also can function adverbially.

affix A morpheme that must be bound to a base to form a word. In English affixes are either prefixes or suffixes.

affricate A type of obstruent that begins with two articulators forming occlusion. The articulators are then released more gradually than they are for the production of stops, resulting in a narrow constriction that produces turbulence as the air stream passes through it. English has two affricates, /tʃ/ and /dʒ/.

allomorph Any one of the variants of a morpheme. All morphemes must have at least one allomorph, but most have more than one. For example, the allomorphs of the plural morpheme are [-s],[-z], and [-əz]. Allomorphs frequently occur in complementary distribution.

allophone Any one of the variants of a phoneme. Allophones are the physical realizations of phonemes. All phonemes must have at least one allophone, but most have more than one. For example, some of the allophones of /t/ are [t], [t˺], and [tʰ]. Allomorphs frequently occur in complementary distribution.

alveolar A point of articulation involving the tip or blade of the tongue and the alveolar ridge. Sounds produced at this point of articulation are alveolars. English has seven alveolar sounds such as /s/, /z/, /t/, /d/, /n/, /r/, and /l/.

alveolar ridge The bony ridge behind the upper front teeth. An important point of articulation for consonants in English.

alveopalatal A point of articulation involving the blade of the tongue and the area between the alveolar ridge and the palate. Sounds produced at this point of articulation are alveopalatals. English has four alveopalatal sounds.

assimilation   The process by which a segment acquires a phonetic feature from a following segment.   For example, vowels become nasalized before nasals in American English

auxiliary verb   Verbs that come before the main verb to form verb groups.   English has three types of auxiliaries: the modals, the primary auxiliaries (*have* and *be*), and the dummy auxiliary, *do*.

base   The morphological structure to which further affixes may be bound.   In the word, *unhappy*, the base is *happy*, but in the word *unhappily* the base is *unhappy*.

bilabial   A point of articulation in which both lips form occlusion.   All sounds made with this type of occlusion are also called bilabials.   More systematically such sounds may also be called labio-labials.   English has three bilabials: /b/, /p/, and /m/.

bound morpheme   A morpheme that must be attached to another morpheme in order for its meaning to become manifest (e.g., the plural morpheme as in *books*).

closed class   A lexical category that does not commonly add new words such as the categories of determiners and coordinating conjunctions.

closed syllable   A syllable that contains a coda.   The monosyllabic word 'seat'--/sit/--consists of a single closed syllable.

coda   A constituent of the syllable consisting of all consonant sounds after the nucleus.   In the word 'beast' the coda is [st].

complementary distribution   The most common manner for the distribution of allophones and allomorphs. Allophones and allomorphs that are in complementary distribution each occur in a unique phonological environment.   For example, the plural morpheme has three allomorphs: [-s],[-z], and [-əz].   The first occurs after voiceless sounds that are not sibilants; the second occurs after voiced sounds that are not sibilants; and the last occurs after all sibilants.   These three environments are mutually exclusive (i.e. they do not overlap).

complex sentence   Any sentence consisting of an independent clause and one or more subordinate clauses.

complex transitive Any verb requiring both a direct object and object complement to complete the predicate.   Also, any clause having this type of verb.

complex word A word consisting of more than one morpheme. *Cat* is not a complex word, but *cats* is.

compound A word composed of two free morphemes such as *blackboard*. Stess is on the first morpheme.

constituent Any unit that is a component of a larger structure. Words are the constituents of phrases, and phrases are the constituents of clauses.

contrastive Two segments contrast if they produced a change in meaning when occurring in the same environment (e.g., the initial sounds in the words feet and beet contrast because they produce different meanings).

coordinating conjunction A lexical category consisting of words that conjoin phrases of equal syntactic structure and equal grammatical function.

copula The verb, *be*, when used as a main verb and not as an auxiliary as in 'Today is Monday.'

degree adverb A type of premodifier. Degree adverbs modify gradable adjectives (*quite smart*) and general adverbs (*very astutely*).

deletion A manipulation that can be used to find some of the phrasal constituents of a sentence and their grammatical functions. Any syntactic structure that can be deleted from a sentence is an optional modifier.

derivational morpheme An affix that may change the lexical category of the base to which it is bound (e.g., *kick* is a verb, but *kick-er* is a noun). Derivational affixes may be either prefixes or suffixes in English.

determiner A functional category whose members co-occur with nouns to form noun phrases. Determiners occur in prenominal position. Articles, demonstratives, and possessive determiners are three sub-categories of determiners.

direct object The noun phrase acting as the complement of a transitive verb.

distinctive Capable to changing meaning. Any linguistic feature that enables a contrast is distinctive.

distinctive feature Any phonetic feature capable of distinguishing one phoneme from another. Voicing is a distinctive feature in English because it is the only feature that distinguishes such pairs of phonemes as /s/ and /z/.

ditransitive Any verb requiring both a direct object and indirect object as complements. Also, any clause having this type of verb.

finite subordinate clause Non-independent clauses that have a tensed verb group. The four finite subordinate clauses in English are adjective clauses, adverb clauses, noun clauses, and *that* clauses.

form class A subdivision of lexical categories. It includes the categories of words that can be identified by their morphological form. These word classes include nouns verbs, adjectives, and to a lesser extent adverbs.

form/function An important distinction in syntactic analysis. The syntactic structure of phrases (the form) can be captured in rules. For example, noun phrases can have the following form (det) (adj) N (pp). However, once phrases are placed in a larger syntactic structure such as a clause, they then perform a grammatical function within that clause. In the sentence 'Books in linguistics are usually expensive' the noun phrase 'books in linguistics' performs the grammatical function of subject of verb, but the same phrase by form performs the grammatical function of direct object in the following sentence: 'The general public does not read books in linguistics.'

free morpheme A morpheme that can be a word without any other morphemes being bound to it (e.g., *house*).

free variation A type of distribution in which more than one allophone can occur in the same phonological environment. For example, in absolute word final position a voiceless stop may be released or unreleased. The final sound in *stop* may therefore be pronounced as [p] or [p¬].

fricative A type of obstruent produced by two articulators forming a constriction radical enough to produce friction as the air stream flows through it. English has nine fricatives such as /f/, /v/, /s/, /z/, and /h/.

functional category A lexical class whose members specify grammatical relationships rather than carry strong semantic content. Functional categories include determiners, coordinating conjunctions, degree adverbs, and subordinating conjunctions).

glide A type of sonorant produced by two articulators forming a constriction large enough to prevent turbulent airflow as the air stream passes through it. Glides are always associated with a vowel either occurring immediately before it as in /ju/ and /wi/ or immediately after as in /aj/ and /kaw/. English has two glides /w/ and /j/.

glottal A point of articulation in which the two vocal folds form a constriction. Sounds produced at this point of articulation are glottals. /h/ is the only glottal sound in English.

glottis The space between the vocal folds.

gradable adjective See **adjective**.

homophones Two words that sound identical but have different meanings. The words *bear* and the *bare* are homophones. Morphemes may also be homophonous as are the comparative and agentive suffixes in *bigg-er* and *runn-er*.

homorganic A term applied to the place of articulation of adjacent obstruents. Adjacent obstruents are homorganic if they have the same place of articulation. The obstruents in the /st/ of /stip/ are homorganic because they are both alveolar.

independent clause A clause that has a tensed verb group, but does not begin with a subordinator, so 'this sentence is an example' is an independent clause, but 'if this sentence were an example' is not independent. All simple sentences consist of one independent clause.

indirect object One of two complements demanded by ditranstive verbs. Thematically, the indirect object designates the benefactive. When indirect objects move to a position after the direct object, they are marked with either *to* or *for* depending upon the ditranstive verb in the clause.

infix An affix that occurs within a base, found in such languages as Bontoc and Tagalog. English does not have any infixes.

inflectional morpheme A group of eight suffixes in English that do not change the lexical category of the stem they are bound to (e.g., boy and boys).

intensive Any verb requiring a subject complement to complete the predicate. Also, any clause having this type of verb.

intransitive Any verb that does not require a complement to complete the predicate (e.g., *die* and *faint*). Also, any clause having this type of verb.

interdental A point of articulation in which the tip of the tongue forms a radical constriction with the upper front teeth, resulting in turbulence as the air stream passes through the constriction. Sounds produced at this point of articulation are interdentals. English has two interdental sounds, /θ/ and /ð/.

intonation The pitch contour over a series of words. Intonation can be contrastive in that a change of intonation over the same string of words can produce a change in meaning.

labial velar A coarticulation in which a sound if formed by constrictions at both the lips and velum. English has one labial velar sound, /w/.

labialization The process by which sounds become round before another round sound.

labio-dental A point of articulation in which the upper front teeth form a narrow constriction with the lower lip. Sounds produced at this point of articulation are labio-dentals. English has two labio-dentals /f/ and /v/.

larynx The cartilaginous structure between the trachea and the pharynx that houses the vocal folds.

lax vowels Vowels that are produced with less tensing of the tongue and less constriction of the vocal tract. In English most lax vowels do not occur in open syllables.

lexical category The word classes that carry strong semantic content rather than indicating grammatical relationships. These categories include nouns, verbs, and adverbs and adjectives.

lexicon The mental dictionary of the speaker of a language.

liquid A type of sonorant produced by two articulators forming a constriction large enough to prevent turbulent airflow as the air stream passes through it. English has two liquids /r/ and /l/.

minimal pair Two words that differ in one and only one sound that is found in the same position in both words (e.g., *pot* and *hot* constitute a minimal pair, but *pot* and *top* to not). Minimal pairs reveal the contrast segments (phonemes) of a language.

monotransitive Any verb requiring a direct object as complement. Also, any clause having this type of verb.

morpheme The minimal unit of meaning or grammatical function in a language. Morphemes may be free or bound and bind together to form complex words.

movement A manipulation in which phrases can be moved from one part of a clause to another; 'Most people rise later during the holidays'; During the holidays most people rise later.' Movement is especially useful for identifying syntactic structures functioning adverbially.

nasal A type of sonorant sound produced by the release of velic closure, resulting in the escape of air through the nasal passage. English has three nasals: /n/, /n/ and /ŋ/.

nasal cavity The chamber above the oral cavity extending from the nostrils to the pharynx.

nasalization The process by which sounds that are normally oral are produced with velic opening. In American English, all vowels before nasals become nasalized.

nominal A functional category. Noun phrases have six grammatical functions in English: subject of verb, subject complement, direct object, indirect object, object complement, and object of preposition. Any syntactic structure that performs any of these grammatical functions is a nominal, so noun phrases, pronouns, noun clauses, and some *that* clauses are nominals. In addition, certain non-finite structures such as infinitive clauses and gerund phrases may be nominals. Pronouns can substitute for any syntactic structure functioning nominally.

non-distinctive feature Any phonetic feature of a segment that is not contrastive. Aspiration, for example, is a phonetic feature of English, but segments with aspiration do not contrast with those without aspiration.

noun One of the four form classes. The three basic types of nouns in English are count nouns, non-count nouns, and proper nouns. *Count nouns* can be preceded by a numeral and be pluralized (*ten students*). *Non-count nouns* cannot be preceded by a numeral and cannot be pluralized (*ten hastes). *Proper nouns* refer to specific entities and cannot be preceded by a numeral or be pluralized.

noun clause A finite subordinate clause that can perform any of the nominal functions. Noun clauses begin with a complementizer such as *whether*, **whoever**, and *whatever*.

noun phrase A noun and all of its modifiers, if any. Pronouns substitute for noun phrases.

non-gradable adjective See **adjective**.

nucleus The sonority peak of the syllable and the only obligatory constituent of a syllable. The segment comprising the nucleus is almost always a vowel, but English permits nasals and liquids to act as the nucleus in unstressed syllables. In the word 'beast' the nucleus is [i].

object complement One of the two complements in a verb phrase headed by a complex transitive verb. The subject complement always follows the first complement, the direct object. In he following sentence, the object complements is unethical: 'Even members of his own party called Richard Nixon unethical at the end of the Watergate investigation.' Noun phrases, adjective phrases, adverb phrases, and prepositional phrases may constitute the object complement.

object marker The words *to* and *for* used to mark the indirect object when it occurs after the direct object.

object of preposition The noun phrase that is the complement of the preposition. Together the two form the prepositional phrase.

obligatory constituent Any phrase that cannot be deleted from a clause without rendering the remaining structure ungrammatical is an obligatory constituent. In the sentence "The books for the biology class are very expensive," the noun phrase, 'the books for the biology class' is obligatory. If it is deleted from the sentence, the remainder is an ungrammatical sentence: *'are very expensive.' Noun phrases are almost always obligatory constituents as are any other syntactic structures performing a nominal function.

obstruent Any consonant that is produced with enough obstruction in the oral cavity to produce friction. All stops, affricates, and fricatives are obstruents.

onset A constituent of the syllable consisting of all consonant sounds before the nucleus. In the word 'beast' the onset is [b].

open class A lexical category that commonly adds new words such as the categories of nouns and verbs.

open syllable A syllable that does not have a coda. The word see--/si/ consists of a single open syllable.

optional constituent Any structure that can be deleted from a greater structure without rendering the latter ungrammatical.

palatal A point of articulation involving the body of the tongue and the palate. Sounds produced at this point of articulation are palatals. The only palatal sound in English is the glide /j/.

palate The hard bony structure in the roof of mouth behind the alveolar ridge and in front of the velum.

passive A type of clause in which the subject of the verb is not the agent of the action. Passive sentences also have a unique verb group--the auxiliary, *be,* followed by the main verb in past participle form. Passive sentences and their active counterparts have different grammatical structures but are synonymous: 'The cat killed the rat' as opposed to 'The rat was killed by the cat.'

pharynx The tubular cavity above the larynx.

pharyngeal A point of articulation formed by the back of the tongue approaching or touching the pharyngeal wall. Sounds produced at this point of articulation are pharyngeals. English does not have any pharyngeal sounds.

phoneme The distinctive sound segments of a language. Phonemes contrast with one another in the same environment. The **minimal pair**, *let* and **bet**, reveals that /l/ and /b/ are two phonemes of English.

phonetic feature Phonetic properties of segments that distinguish one segment from another. Examples of phonetic features are nasal, alveolar, voiced, and interdental.

phrasal constituent Any phrase that is a component of a larger syntactic structure. The short sentence 'English grammar is interesting' has two phrasal constituents, the noun phrase 'English grammar' and the verb phrase 'is interesting.' Phrasal constituents are important because they can be manipulated, and they acquire a grammatical function once they are in a larger grammatical structure.

pitch The perceived auditory sensation produced by the frequency with which the vocal cords vibrate, the greater the frequency of vibration, the higher the pitch.

predicate adverb Adverbs that occur only in the predicate of a clause.

prefix An affix that is attached to the beginning of a base. The prefix in the word unhappy is {-un}.

preposition A functional category whose members generally convey information about place and time such as *on* and *before*; however, others are nearly devoid of semantic content such as *of*. The preposition serves as the head of the prepositional phrase.

prepositional phrase A phrase composed of the head preposition and a following complement called the object of preposition. The object is almost always a noun phrase. Though prepositional phrases must always have both the preposition and the object to be grammatical, the object may under certain circumstances be moved to a position before the head.

proform Normally a single word that can substitute for an entire phrase. English has a number of different types of proforms. As examples, pronouns substitute for noun phrases; then and there substitute for different phrases of time and place; the first auxiliary of a verb group can substitute for an entire verb phrase, and a possessive pronoun can substitute specifically for a NP with a possessive determiner in it.

pronoun A closed lexical class that bears such semantic properties as number, person, and gender. Some types of English pronouns are subject pronouns, object pronouns, reflexive pronouns, possessive pronouns and relative pronouns. Pronouns substitute for noun phrases.

rhyme The nucleus and the coda taken together as a unit in opposition to the onset. In the word scream, phonemically /skrim/, /skr/ is the onset and /im/ is the rhyme. Rhymes are important in determining the weight of a syllable.

root The morpheme that remains after all affixes have been removed. In the word *un-happi-ly*, the root is *happy*.

sentence adverb Adverbs that modify the contents of an entire clause. They may occur at the beginning of the clause or in the predicate: 'Normally, students do well in linguistics'; 'Students normally do well in linguistics'; 'Students do well in linguistics normally.'

simple sentence A sentence that consists of a single finite clause.

simple word A word consisting of one free morpheme. All free morphemes are simple words.

sonorant Any sound produced with too little constriction between the articulators to form turbulence as the air stream flows through. Nasals, liquids, and glides are all sonorants.

sonority The natural loudness of a sound when stress, length, and pitch are held constant. Sonority is related to the degree of constriction between two articulators, the greater the constriction the lower the sonority. Though somewhat elusive to define, sonority is a valuable concept for describing the structure of syllables.

stem The lexical item to which an inflectional morpheme is attached (e.g., *decision* is the stem of *decisions*).

stop A type of obstruent formed by occlusion at some point in the oral cavity. Air pressure builds up behind the occlusion, and the articulators involved in forming the occlusion are released suddenly allowing the air to escape. English has six oral stops: /p/, /t/, /k/, /b/, /d/, and /g/. The nasals may also be considered stops because occlusion occurs in the oral cavity. However, the air is released through the nasal cavity, not the oral cavity. Because of this difference, the nasals can be referred to as nasal stops.

stress The use of extra respiratory energy in the production of some syllables. The result is that stressed syllables in English are longer, louder, and higher in pitch. In Spanish stressed syllables are louder and higher in pitch, but not longer.

stress-timing A type of rhythm in which the amount of stress on a syllable determines its length. English is a stress-timed language.

subject complement The complement following an intensive verb. Four different types of phrases can constitute the subject complement: noun phrase, adjective phrase, adverb phrase, and prepositional phrase.

subject of verb A phonological unit usually consisting of more than one segment. A syllable must always have a nucleus, the sonority peak of the syllable, which is normally comprised a vowel. Syllables may contain two further constituents, an onset consisting of all consonants before the nucleus and a coda consisting of all consonants after the nucleus.

substitution A manipulation in which single words take the place of entire phrases. **Pronouns**, for example, substitute for noun phrases or for any other structure with a nominal function. Single words used in substitution are called proforms, pronouns being just one type of proform. Two other proforms are *then* and *there*; they can substitute for adverbials of time and place respectively.

suffix An affix that is attached to the end of a base. The suffix in *establishment* is {-ment}.

syllable A phonological unit usually consisting of more than one segment. A syllable must always have a nucleus, the sonority peak of the syllable, which is normally comprised a vowel. Syllables may contain two further constituents, an onset consisting of all consonants before the nucleus and a coda consisting of all consonants after the nucleus.

syllable-timing A type of rhythm in which all syllables have approximately the same length regardless of the amount of stress on the syllables. Spanish is a syllable-timed language.

tense vowels Vowels produced with a relative greater tensing of the tongue and a consequent greater constriction of the vocal tract. In English the four tensed simple vowels are /i/, /e/, /o/, and /u/.

that **clause** A finite subordinate clause that begins with the complementizer *that*. That clauses are versatile in English having nominal functions as well as being post modifiers of nouns and adjectives.

tone The contrastive pitch contour over syllables. A change in tone over the same syllable produces a change in meaning. Chinese is a tone language; English is not.

transitive Any verb requiring a direct object. Monotransitive, ditransitive, and complex transitive verbs are all transitives though the latter two types of verbs have complements in addition to the direct object.

uvula The soft muscular tissue that dangles from the back of the velum.

uvular A point of articulation in which the back of the tongue forms a constriction or articulation with the uvula. Sounds produced at this point of articulation are uvulars. English does not have any uvular sounds.

velar A point of articulation in which the back of the tongue form a constriction or occlusion with the velum. Sounds produced at this point of articulation are velars. English has three velar sounds: /k/, /g/, and /ŋ/.

velic closure The raising of the velum against the pharyngeal wall forcing the air stream to exit through the oral cavity. All oral sounds are produced with velic closure.

velic opening The lowering of the velum away from the pharyngeal wall which allows the air stream to exit through the nasal cavity.

velum The area of soft muscular tissue behind the palate.

verb One of the four form classes. Any word in English that is inflected for tense is a verb. Regular verbs take the four inflectional endings; the third person singular (*walks*), the past tense (*walked*), the present participle (*walking*), and the past participle (*walked*). Verbs are always the head of a verb phrase.

verb group A main verb and all of its auxiliaries if any. The verb group must consist of at least the main verb; it may have up to three auxiliary verbs.

verb phrase A main verb and all its auxiliaries, complements, and modifiers, if any. The verb phrase also performs the grammatical function and predicate in a clause.

voiced The vocal quality produced through the vibration of the vocal folds. The sound [z] is voiced.

voiceless The vocal quality produced by the lack of vibration of the vocal folds. The sound [s] is voiceless.

word A minimal free form in a language. All simple words are composed of exactly one free morpheme.

word stress The stress that occurs on a syllable in an individual word. Word stress is contrastive; if the fist syllable of *conflict* is stressed, the word is a noun, but if the second syllable is stressed, it is a verb.

zero relative pronoun When the relative pronoun in an adjective clause is not the subject in its own clause, it may be deleted from the surface of the sentence. This deleted pronoun is called the zero relative pronoun. In this sentence the relative pronoun is *that*: 'The students read the article that the instructor recommended.' Because *that* is not the subject in its own clause, it may be deleted: 'The students read the article [0] the instructor recommended.'